The Twine Cookbook

First Edition

This work is licensed under the Creative Commons Attribution-ShareAlike 4.0 International License. To view a copy of this license, visit http://creativecommons.org/licenses/by-sa/4.0/ or send a letter to Creative Commons, PO Box 1866, Mountain View, CA 94042, USA.

The material used in this book was adapted from the online version of the Twine Cookbook, which was authored by Daniel Cox, Chris Klimas, Thomas Michael Edwards, David Tarrant, Leon Arnott, Shawn Graham, Akjosch, Chapel, G.C. "Grim" Baccaris, Evelyn Mitchell, and James Skemp. For more information and to access the online Cookbook or download a PDF of this book, visit **https://twinery.org/cookbook/**

Significant technical assistance in the content adaptation provided by Mary DeMarco.

Layout and cover art by Rae Yung.

Funding for this edition comes from the Interactive Fiction Technology Foundation.

Table of Contents

9	**Introduction**	**38**	**Working with HTML**
10	Foreword	39	Reviewing HTML
13	Using the Twine Cookbook	43	Chapbook HTML
14	Style Guide	45	Harlowe HTML
		47	SugarCube HTML
15	**Common Questions**	50	Snowman HTML
16	How do I get started?		
17	What do I need to know?	**52**	**Working with CSS**
18	How do I style text?	53	Reviewing CSS Selectors
19	Where are my stories saved?	56	Chapbook CSS
		59	Harlowe CSS
20	**Common Terms**	61	SugarCube CSS
21	Cookbook	63	Snowman CSS
21	CSS		
22	HTML	**66**	**Working with JavaScript**
24	JavaScript	67	Reviewing JavaScript
25	Macros	68	Chapbook JavaScript
26	Markdown / Markup	70	Harlowe JavaScript
27	Passages	71	SugarCube JavaScript
28	Stories	72	Snowman JavaScript
29	Story Formats		
31	Twee	**74**	**Twine 2 Examples**
35	Twine		
35	Variables		

Twine Cookbook

Chapbook

76	Adding Functionality
77	Arrays
78	Audio
79	Conditional Statements
80	CSS and Passage Tags
81	Cycling Choices
82	Date and Time
83	Delayed Text
84	Deleting Variables
85	Dice Rolling
86	Dropdown
87	Fairmath System
89	Geolocation
92	Google Fonts
93	Headers and Footers
94	Images
96	Importing External JavaScript
99	Keyboard Events
101	Lock and Key: Variable
103	Looping
104	Passages in Passages
105	Passage Visits
106	Player Statistics
109	Setting and Showing Variables

Harlowe

130	Arrays
131	Conditional Statements
132	CSS Selectors
135	CSS and Passage Tags
136	Cycling Choices
137	Date and Time
138	Delayed Text
139	Dice Rolling
140	Dropdown
141	Fairmath System
143	Geolocation
146	Google Fonts
147	Headers and Footers
148	Hidden Link
151	Images
153	Importing External JavaScript
155	Keyboard Events
157	Left Sidebar
159	Lock and Key: Variable
161	Looping
162	Modal (Pop-up Window)
164	Modularity
165	Moving through a dungeon
169	Passages in Passages
170	Passage Transitions
171	Passage Visits
172	Player Statistics
175	Programmatic Undo
176	Saving Games
177	Setting and Showing Variables

Snowman

198	Adding Functionality
199	Arrays
201	Audio
202	Conditional Statements
203	CSS Selectors
205	CSS and Passage Tags
206	Cycling Choices
209	Date and Time
210	Delayed Text
211	Deleting Variables
212	Dice Rolling
214	Fairmath System
216	Geolocation
220	Google Fonts
221	Headers and Footers
222	Hidden Link
224	Images
226	Importing External JavaScript
228	Keyboard Events
230	Left Sidebar
232	Lock and Key: Variable
234	Looping
236	Modal (Pop-up Window)
239	Modularity
240	Moving through a dungeon
244	Passage Events
246	Passages in Passages
247	Render Passage to Element
248	Passage Transitions
249	Passage Visits
250	Player Statistics
254	Programmatic Undo
255	Saving Games
258	Setting and Showing Variables

SugarCube

283	Adding Functionality
284	Arrays
286	Audio
288	Conditional Statements
289	CSS Selectors
291	CSS and Passage Tags
293	Cycling Choices
295	Date and Time
296	Delayed Text
297	Deleting Variables
298	Dice Rolling
299	Fairmath System
301	Geolocation
305	Google Fonts
306	Headers and Footers
307	Hidden Link
309	Images
311	Importing External JavaScript
313	Keyboard Events
315	Left Sidebar
317	Loading Screen
318	Lock and Key: Variable
320	Looping
321	Modal (Pop-up Window)
322	Modularity
324	Moving through a dungeon
327	Passage Events
329	Passages in Passages
330	Render Passage to Element
331	Passage Transitions
332	Passage Visits
333	Player Statistics
336	Programmatic Undo
337	Saving Games
339	Setting and Showing Variables

Chapbook

110	Space Exploration
117	Static Healthbars
118	Story and Passage API
119	Style Markup
121	Timed Passages
122	Turn Counter
125	Typewriter Effect
127	Variable Story Styling

Harlowe

178	Space Exploration
183	Static Healthbars
184	Storylets
187	Style Markup
189	Timed Passages
191	Turn Counter
193	Typewriter Effect
195	Variable Story Styling

Snowman

259	Space Exploration
265	Static Healthbars
266	Story and Passage API
267	Style Markup
269	Timed Passages
271	Timed Progress Bars
276	Turn Counter
279	Typewriter Effect
281	Variable Story Styling

SugarCube

340	Space Exploration
345	Static Healthbars
346	Story and Passage API
347	Style Markup
348	Templates
349	Timed Passages
351	Timed Progress Bars
356	Turn Counter
358	Typewriter Effect
359	Variable Story Styling
360	Using Add-ons

Introduction

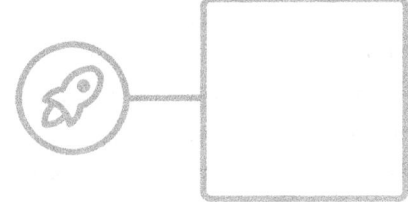

Foreword

Writer or programmer? I've struggled with this question for a long time. It began as a personal one, but became central to the concept of Twine.

The two identities seemed at odds with each other to me at first, and I thought I had to choose just one. I pictured writers as intuitive, emotional people, and programmers as logical and exact. These weren't ideas that I invented. I absorbed them from the culture around me, but I didn't think of it that way. It was instead an unsolvable problem, because I felt tugged in both directions equally. I remember now, twenty years later, the befuddlement my undergrad advisor displayed when I explained I wanted to take classes in both Shakespeare and data structures one semester. But that's what I wanted. (To his credit, he never tried to talk me out of it.)

Over time, I realized that this question of writer or programmer was unsolvable because the question itself was incorrect. None of us have just one identity. I'm both a writer and programmer—and many other things besides. Identity is complex and sometimes seemingly contradictory. There are intuitive programmers and precise writers.

Twine has a similarly complex nature. You can make stories with Twine and you can make games with Twine. You can also make poems, simulations, personal essays, puzzles, and comics. You also can make things that defy easy explanation at all. I love this aspect of Twine. I love how difficult it is to categorize the things made with it, just as you cannot categorize the people who use Twine. They are writers and they are programmers. They are experts and they are beginners. They are complex and contradictory.

Part of the reason why the Twine community is vibrant and hard-to-pin-down are story formats. Early in Twine's history, story formats were similar to themes: each format behaved more-or-less identically, but varied in the appearance of content onscreen. But as what people have wanted to do with Twine evolved, so did story formats. They are now more like domain-specific languages, each with their own point of view, and accordingly, their own strengths and weaknesses. Story formats have added things that were never part of my original design for Twine, from HTML5-based audio to storylet-based narrative structures.

With choice comes complexity. Just like human languages, it's not easy or fast to change to another story format once you've gotten some experience with one, and when you need help doing something, you'll probably be most successful talking to people who are using that same language. This can be frustrating, especially for new authors who may not even know what a story format is in the first place.

Daniel Cox had the insight to recognize this complexity, and the determination to address it by creating the first edition of the Twine Cookbook. This book would not exist if not for all of his work, and that of the many community members who contributed to it under his editorial leadership.

Daniel's vision was part Rosetta Stone, part tutorial, and part—well, cookbook. Here, you'll find descriptions of tasks that Twine authors often want to do paired with detailed descriptions and full code examples for the most common Twine story formats. Just like cooking recipes, these can be used without alteration and yield successful results, but they can also be used as jumping-off points for experimentation. For example, the Turn Counter section describes how to map the number of passages a reader has visited to a 24-hour clock, to approximate time passing as the reader progresses through the story. But your story may need to track time in a slightly different way. If so, you can adapt the code you'll find there for your own purposes.

This is where I think the Cookbook shines. It would be impossible to cover every possible thing you'd want to do with Twine, but the Cookbook can give you the first few steps of whatever path you wish to take as an author.

While you could read this book cover-to-cover, you most likely will be best-served by skipping to the examples that seem most interesting, or skimming through the sections to see what draws your eye. Even if you don't have a particular problem that needs solving right now, reading through the examples might inspire some ideas in your own work.

You can also use this Cookbook as way to explore other story formats. If you're wondering if a particular story format would be a good fit for a project, try taking a look at the examples for a task you already understand how to do. They can help you understand a format's particular idiom.

The Cookbook's home is **https://twinery.org/cookbook**. It is a living resource that any Twine community member can contribute to, whether it be a new recipe or a correction or improvement on an existing one. Just as story formats have evolved, so does the Cookbook. This print edition serves as a snapshot, a record of a constantly-changing thing. But practically speaking, this edition also exists for all the reasons that one might prefer print to the web, even in the 2020s. It exists for people who do not have ready internet access; for classrooms, physical and otherwise; and for those who simply prefer to keep reference books at hand on a desk instead of in a browser tab.

The Cookbook has been a bedrock of the Twine community. It's the first place I look when I have a question, and the first place I point new authors who want to understand how to build things with Twine. I hope it will prove as useful to you.

Chris Klimas
June 2024

Using the Twine Cookbook

On each example page under the different topic areas, the *Twine Cookbook* provides examples, Twee source code, and links to download either.

Downloading and Using the Examples

1. Download the compiled HTML from an example page.
2. Import the file into Twine.
   - Twine 2: Use the "Import From File" link on the right-hand side under the "+Story" button.
   - Twine 1: Use the File>Import menu option and select "Compiled HTML File…".

Downloading and Using Twee Code

Twee source code is provided for all examples to more easily show the passages and what they contain.

Twine 2

Twine 2 can import Twee source code by choosing Library>Import from the story list.

Twine 1

For Twine 1 examples, the Twee source code can be downloaded and imported through going to File>Import and selecting "Twee Source Code…".

Style Guide

The Twine Cookbook uses certain conventions to indicate that pieces of text should be considered as macros, part of JavaScript, or values to be used with either.

All variables are highlighted with *emphasis*. If a Story Format provides or an example uses particular JavaScript functionality, it will appear with **strong emphasis**.

Example:

> This example uses the variable *exampleValue* and uses the global object **window** and function **parseInt()**.

In some cases, the value of a variable is shown in quotation marks. This is to help users see which values are used and how they might be transformed or inform certain functionality.

Common Questions

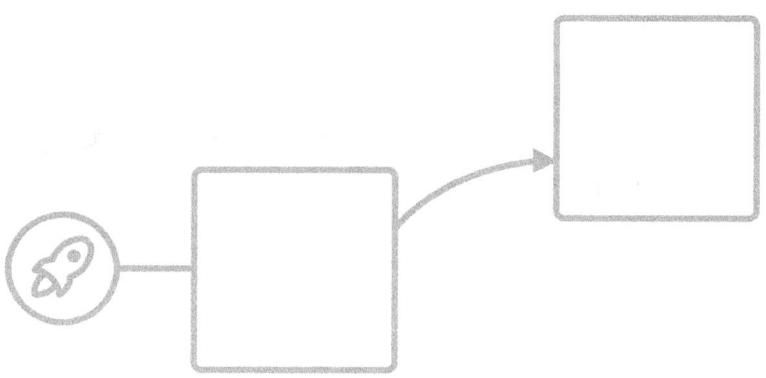

How do I get started?

Online

Twine 2 can be accessed online at **https://twinery.org/2**. You can create and publish Twine projects without having to download anything using the online version.

Offline

Twine 2 can also be downloaded and run on Windows, MacOS, and Linux systems. The latest releases on GitHub has a listing of the current versions per operating system.

Twine 1

Twine 1 is only a desktop application. While it can still be used, it is not currently maintained or under active development. The current version is 1.4.2.

What do I need to know?

Nothing!

You can make a game, interactive project, or experimental essay without knowing programming or anything other than how to navigate a program and publish HTML using Twine 2!

However, getting the most out of Twine 2 often requires some knowledge of HTML, CSS, or JavaScript. All of the Story Formats also use markup to style text.

HTML, CSS, and JavaScript

The *Twine Cookbook* has entries on HTML, CSS, and JavaScript as they are used in connection with Twine 2.

Markup

All of the built-in Story Formats use different ways of marking up text in order to add some visual *emphasis* or otherwise **style the text**. These differ between Story Formats, and it is highly recommended to consult the individual documentation of a Story Format for more information and examples.

How do I style text?

Each Story Format uses its own markup and special characters to format text. Some common examples are included below.

Story Format	Emphasis	Strong Emphasis	Verbatim Text
Chapbook	`*Italics*` or `_Italics_`	`__Bold__` or `**Bold**`	Any text following a new line and four spaces or a tab until the end of the line.
Harlowe	`*Italics*` or `//Italics//`	`**Bold**` or `''Bold''`	`Verbatim`
Snowman	`*Italics*`	`**Bold**`	Any text following a new line and four spaces or a tab until the end of the line.
SugarCube	`//Italics//`	`''Bold''`	`"""Verbatim"""` or `<nowiki>Verbatim</nowiki>`

See **page 118** for more information on **Chapbook markup**

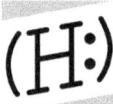

See **page 186** for more information on **Harlowe markup**

See **page 266** for more information on **Snowman markup**

See **page 346** for more information on **SugarCube markup**

Where are my stories saved?

Twine 2

Online

Stories are saved in the local storage of a web browser. This is isolated between a browser and its use of incognito or private windows. *Clearing sessions and cookies in a browser may also clear the storage of Twine 2.* Using a different browser also means accessing different local storage.

Desktop

When used as a desktop application, Twine 2 stores its files under the current user's files. The current collection of Stories can be accessed through the View -> Show Story Library menu option.

Twine 1

As a desktop application, Twine 1 stores its files in either HTML or as Twee source code on the local computer. It can import and export both HTML and Twee source code (`.twee` or `.tw`).

Common Terms

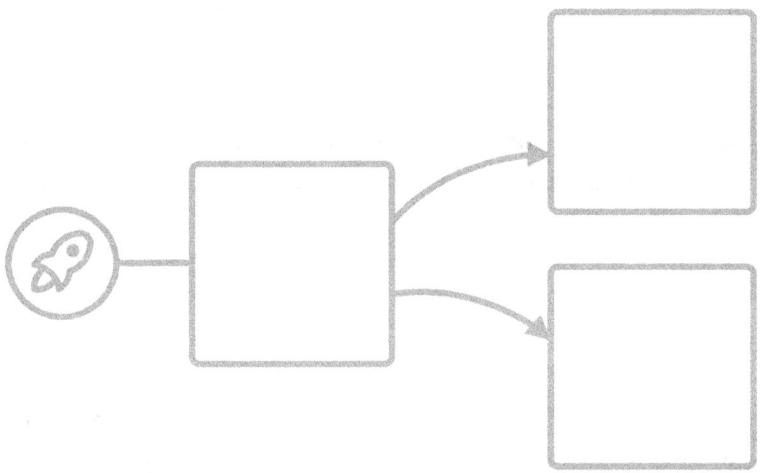

Cookbook

The idea for a *Twine Cookbook* was heavily inspired by the *Inform Recipe Book*, a collection of examples to learn Inform. Our original editorial team sought to create the same project for Twine by compiling some of the most requested code solutions across multiple versions, histories, and even years of development. After publishing the first version in August 2017, the *Twine Cookbook* was born.

What this is

The *Twine Cookbook* is a living document. It has rolling deadlines and is often updated multiple times a year as new requests and solutions to old problems are found and submitted. It is driven by the Twine community and finds inspiration in what others create and share online.

CSS

Cascading Style Sheets (CSS) is programming language for describing the presentation of HTML elements (*i.e.* the colors, fonts, spacing, and general layout of a web page). "Cascading" means rules move from a parent element to any children. Any specific rules also overrule any general ones.

CSS styles are associated with HTML elements using the element's (tag)name, id, classes, and/or other, possibly custom, attributes. Each built-in Story Format in Twine 2 uses different, sometimes custom, HTML elements to organize the Story and then applies its own CSS rules.

Story Stylesheet

When using Twine, additional CSS rules can be added through the Story Stylesheet screen. This CSS is inserted into the final Story and provides an opportunity to override the color and formatting choices expressed in the Story Format's own stylesheet. (When using Twee, styles can be added using one or more passages tagged "stylesheet".)

Considering the complex nature of CSS cascading, it is always highly recommended to use a Story Format's own macros where possible to change the presentation or layout of a story.

Common areas involved in Story Format styling include the full page or window, a sidebar (if present), and the current passage as a sub-area of the page. Often, there is also a mechanism to style passages according to their tags (as assigned in Twine 2). See the CSS Selectors recipes for more details.

HTML

The HyperText Markup Language (HTML) is the standard for all documents designed for a web browser. It consists of a series of elements which define the structure of a page and the layout of its content.

Story Format Layout

Each Story Format handles its own layout and HTML structure. While CSS can be used to style its elements, it is often recommended to use any existing macros in a Story Format for this purpose, if available.

- Harlowe: Named Hooks
- SugarCube: CSS Selectors
- Snowman: HTML Elements
- Chapbook: Customization

Twine 2 HTML

All data of a Twine 2 Story is stored as a series of HTML elements within a page according to the HTML Output Specification.

Example:

```
<tw-storydata>
  <style
    role="stylesheet"
    id="twine-user-stylesheet"
    type="text/twine-css">
  </style>
  <script
    role="script"
    id="twine-user-script"
    type="text/twine-javascript">
  </script>
  <tw-tag
    name="tagName"
    color="orange">
  </tw-tag>
  <tw-passagedata
      pid="1"
      name="Start"
      tags="tag1 tag2"
      position="102,99"
      size="100,100">
  Some content
  </tw-passagedata>
</tw-storydata>
```

JavaScript

The programming language JavaScript is embedded in all modern web browsers and is a foundational part of how Twine works.

Knowledge of JavaScript is not required to create Stories using Twine. However, understanding how JavaScript works and the expectations of how things are structured in the language can be helpful when using advanced functionality in SugarCube and when using Snowman.

Story JavaScript

When using Twine, extra functionality can be added through the Story JavaScript screen. This is run before the story is run and provides an opportunity to write specialized code or include external libraries and files. Some Story Formats, like SugarCube, provide the ability to translate between JavaScript and macro usage in Twine. Others, like Snowman, expect this to be used when creating more complex projects.

window.setup

Based on the object of the same name provided by SugarCube, the cookbook suggests using or creating a *window.setup* global object when working with Story JavaScript in Twine for greater portability between Story formats.

window.setup Example

```
window.setup = window.setup || {};
```

Macros

Macros allow programming code to be intermixed with text shown onscreen. They allow a wide variety of functionality to be added to a story, from changing the appearance of text to reacting to mouse and touch events. An author's choice of Story Formats is often made based on the macros they provide and how they can be used together.

Twine 1 and SugarCube

In Twine 1, macros were written with two less-than (<<) and two-greater-than signs (>>) around code. (SugarCube, as a successor of this form, follows the same syntax.)

Example:

```
<<display "Another Passage">>
```

Harlowe

The Harlowe Story Format uses a different syntax for macros. They are wrapped in parentheses (()) and use brackets ([]) to indicate which text or sections are associated or acted upon by the macro.

Example:

```
(font: "Arial")[This text will be in Arial.]
```

Snowman

Snowman does not provide macros in the same sense that SugarCube and Harlowe do. It does allow mixing JavaScript code in text with <% and %>, and displaying the results of the code on the page with <%= and %>.

Example:

```
The chalkboard reads 2 + 2 = <%= 2 + 2 %>.
```

Chapbook

Chapbook provides inserts and modifiers to work with variables and other values. However, any variable testing must be done within the vars section itself.

Example:

```
largeFamily: cousins > 10
--
```

Markdown / Markup

All built-in Story Formats use a form of markup.

Markdown

John Gruber and Aaron Swartz created Markdown in 2004 with the goal of creating a way to add extra symbols to plain text in order to easily convert it into HTML. Since then, it has become very popular for text input, with sites like GitHub supporting it.

Snowman and Chapbook use a modified version of Markdown for styling text.

Markup

Harlowe and SugarCube use what is known as markup. To change the presentation of text, extra symbols are added to create visual effects like *emphasis* and **stronger emphasis**. Most wiki software and sites like Wikipedia use markup to style text.

Differences

Markdown *is* markup. It is a way of changing the presentation of text through adding extra symbols that have special meaning when other programs read it and convert it into a different format like HTML. The only real difference is that Markdown has a name whereas "markup" is a category of all languages that perform the same actions.

Passages

Passages can be thought of as divisions of time, space, or combinations of the two. They can also be thought of as blocks of dialogue, sections of code, or simply ways to break up a complicated project into more easily understood parts. In Twine, passages are at the core of any story.

Connecting Passages

The simplest way to connect passages is through adding two opening and closing brackets, `[[ ]]`, around any collection of letters, numbers, or punctuation. If a passage exists with those exact characters in the same ordering and combination, the passages will be linked together. When viewing the compiled HTML version, there will now be a link to navigate between the two.

By default, passage links are one-way. Navigating the link means moving away from one passage to another.

Link to Another Passage named "Link to another passage"

```
[[Link to another passage]]
```

Link to Another Passage Named "Different Passage"

The pipe, "|", can be used to rename a link from its original text to some other name for the same purpose.

```
[[Link to another passage|Different Passage]]
```

Link to Another Passage Named "Different Passage" Using Routing

Starting in Twine 2, arrows (`->` or `<-`) can be used to to route links, *pointing* to the destination of the link.

```
[[Link to another passage->Different Passage]]
[[Different Passage<-Link to another passage]]
```

Stories

Anything made using Twine can be called by any name. They are no rules on naming conventions and everything from experimental games to more traditional novels can be created in Twine. Everything is welcome. In general, the Twine editor calls individual projects stories.

Stories can be published to HTML and are readable in a web browser without Twine. In their published form, they can also be imported into Twine for further editing.

IFID

When created, each story is each given a series of letters and numbers called an Interactive Fiction IDentifier (IFID).

The IFID is always retained when importing or publishing Stories. This helps authors track their projects on different platforms, or know if other authors have copied or tried to claim it as their own without their knowledge or consent.

Story Formats

Each Story Format provides a different visual layout, set of macros, and internal JavaScript functionality. In Twine 1, Story Formats primarily denoted different visual layouts; however, since Twine 2, Story Formats are more like different dialects.

Chapbook

Chapbook is a "second-generation" Twine 2 Story Format that separates its functionality into "inserts", which cause text to appear, and "modifiers", which affect text in some way.

Chapbook Example:

```
[if hasKey]
It looks like the key will open the door.
[else]
No way forward!
```

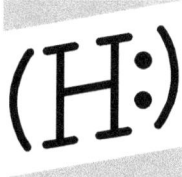

Harlowe

Harlowe is the default Story Format in Twine 2. It is designed for ease-of-use and for those using Twine 2 for the first time.

Harlowe Example:

```
(if: $hasKey)[It looks like the key will open the door.]
(else:)[No way forward!]
```

Snowman

Snowman is designed to be written with custom JavaScript and CSS. It has no built-in macros, but includes the Underscore.js, Marked, and jQuery JavaScript libraries.

Snowman Example:

```
<% if (s.hasKey) { %>
It looks like the key will open the door.
<% } else { %>
No way forward!
<% } %>
```

SugarCube

SugarCube continues the traditions of Twine 1 while also expanding the available macros. It has more functionality than Harlowe, but can sometimes require greater knowledge of programming techniques and development patterns for more advanced usage.

SugarCube Example:

```
<<if $hasKey>>
It looks like the key will open the door.
<<else>>
No way forward!
<</if>>
```

Twee

Twee is the source code of a Twine story. In Twine 1, Stories could be exported into their source, changed, and imported again. Twine 2 has moved away from this functionality, but has been heavily influenced through having sections (passages in Twine 1) where the user can add CSS (Story Stylesheet) and JavaScript (Story JavaScript).

Notation

Starting with Twee 3, there is a standard for reading and writing Twee when working with Twine 2 passages.

Twee 3 notation is written as a series of four parts for the header of each passage:

- Sigil: (Required) Two colons (":") followed by a space
- Passage Name: (Required) The name of the passage
- Tags: (Optional) Optional tags
- Metadata: (Optional) Information about the passage

The content of a passage continues until the next header of a passage is found or the input ends with at least a single empty line between passage headers.

Example Twee Notation:

```
:: Snoopy [dog peanuts]
Snoopy is a dog in the comic Peanuts.

:: Charlie Brown [person peanuts] {"position":"600,400","size":"100,200"}
Charlie Brown is a person in the comic Peanuts
```

Special Passage Names

Some compilers understand and process certain keywords differently. The following is a common set of case-sensitive, reserved passage names across Twine 1 and Twee 3.

Start (Twine 1 and Twee 3)

The first passage in a story.

```
:: Start
A beginning!
```

StoryTitle (Twine 1 and Twee 3)

The title of the story.

```
:: StoryTitle
A Named Story
```

StorySubtitle (Twine 1)

The subtitle of the story.

```
:: StorySubtitle
The subtitle of this story
```

StoryAuthor (Twine 1)

The author of the story.

```
:: StoryAuthor
John Smith
```

StoryMenu (Twine 1)

Corresponds to the menu that hovers or on the left side of the page in the Sugarcane Story Format.

```
:: StoryMenu
Content of the story menu!
```

StorySettings (Twine 1)

Used to specify certain options and settings.

- Undo: Enables the player to "undo moves." In Sugarcane, this means being able to use the Back button in the browser. In Jonah, this means being able to use the "Rewind to here" link, and being able to click links in previous passages.
- Bookmark: Enables the player to use the "Bookmark" link in Sugarcane and Jonah. On by default.
- Hash updates: This causes the current passage's bookmark URL to be automatically placed in the player's browser address bar whenever they change passages. This is off by default because the URLs can become very long and ugly quickly.
- Prompt before closing: If the player tries to reload or close the page, the browser will prompt for confirmation. This is useful for long games - it would be unfortunate if the player lost a lot of progress due to an idle key-press.
- Don't use default CSS: This removes most of the CSS used by the Story Format, allowing CSS programmers to write their own stylesheet redesigns more easily. Off by default - but including the text "blank stylesheet" in a stylesheet will set it on automatically.
- ROT13: Obfuscates the Story's HTML source to dissuade people from spoiling themselves by reading it. Off by default.
- jQuery: Include the library or not.
- Modernizr: Include the the library or not.

```
:: StorySettings
undo:on
bookmark:on
hash:on
exitprompt:on
blankcss:on
obfuscate:rot13
jquery:on
modernizr:on
```

StoryIncludes (Twine 1)

Includes "imports", other local or remote files, during the HTML compilation process. In Twine 1.4.2, both Twine Story (.tws) and Twine Source (.twee) files can be used.

```
:: StoryIncludes
localfile.tws
```

StoryData (Twee 3)

A JSON chunk encapsulating various Twine 2-compatible details about the Story.

- ifid: (Required) IFID of the Story
- format: (Optional) Story Format
- format-version: (Optional) Story Format version
- start: (Optional) PID of starting passage
- tag-colors: (Optional) Pairs of tags and colors
- zoom: (Optional) Decimal zoom level

```
:: StoryData
{
    "ifid": "D674C58C-DEFA-4F70-B7A2-27742230C0FC",
    "format": "SugarCube",
    "format-version": "2.28.2",
    "start": "My Starting Passage",
    "tag-colors": {
        "bar": "green",
        "foo": "red",
        "qaz": "blue"
    },
    "zoom": 0.25
}
```

Special Tag Names

Twee 3 defines two special case-sensitive lowercase passage tags: **stylesheet** and **script**.

(Passages are also loaded according to alphabetical order if others exist with the same special passage tags.)

Stylesheet

Any additional or overriding CSS rules for the Story.

```
:: UserStylesheet[stylesheet]
```

Script

Any additional or overriding JavaScript code for the Story.

```
:: UserScript[script]
```

Twine

Twine is an open-source tool for telling interactive, nonlinear stories. Navigation works by clicking (or, on mobile devices, tapping) on links to change old content, refresh current content, or even load new content.

Making with Twine

Because Twine produces HTML that web browsers can read, the limitations on Twine are not in what can be developed with the tool, but in the web browsers that run it. Anything that can be done in a web browser can be done in Twine.

Variables

In programming terminology, a variable is a container for a value that can change. In Twine, a variable is a way of storing and acting on data of some sort. Anything from a number to a series of characters can be stored in a variable. Unlike other code or text in a Passage, variables most commonly start with either a dollar sign (**$**) or an underscore (**_**) in the Harlowe and SugarCube Story Formats. (In Chapbook, variables are part of a 'vars section'.)

Story Variables (Harlowe and SugarCube)

Once created, story variables in Twine can be accessed from any passage at any time. They are *globally* accessible to all functionalities everywhere.

Example:

```
$numberVariable
```

Variables are translated into their values when used by themselves in a passage. To display their value, they can simply be included as part of any other text.

Example:

```
The value of the variable is $numberVariable.
```

Temporary Variables (Harlowe and SugarCube)

It can often be useful to work with values in a more controlled manner. For this purpose, temporary variables can be used. They are *locally* accessible. They only exist while the current passage is shown. They start with an underscore (_).

Example:

```
_tempVariable
```

Temporary variables can also be used to display their values with other text like Story Variables.

Example:

```
The value of the variable is _numberVariable.
```

Differences in Chapbook

Chapbook handles variables differently. Instead of variables needing to start with the dollar sign (**$**) or an underscore (**_**), Chapbook also allows variable names to start with upper or lowercase letters as well.

Example:

```
strength: 18
$dexterity: 7
_constitution: 14
```

Differences in Snowman

Snowman uses JavaScript variables. It provides three global variables: *window.story* (for working with the story), *window.passage* (for working with the current passage), and *s* (as a way to access values across passages).

Example:

```
s.strength = 14;
```

Working with HTML

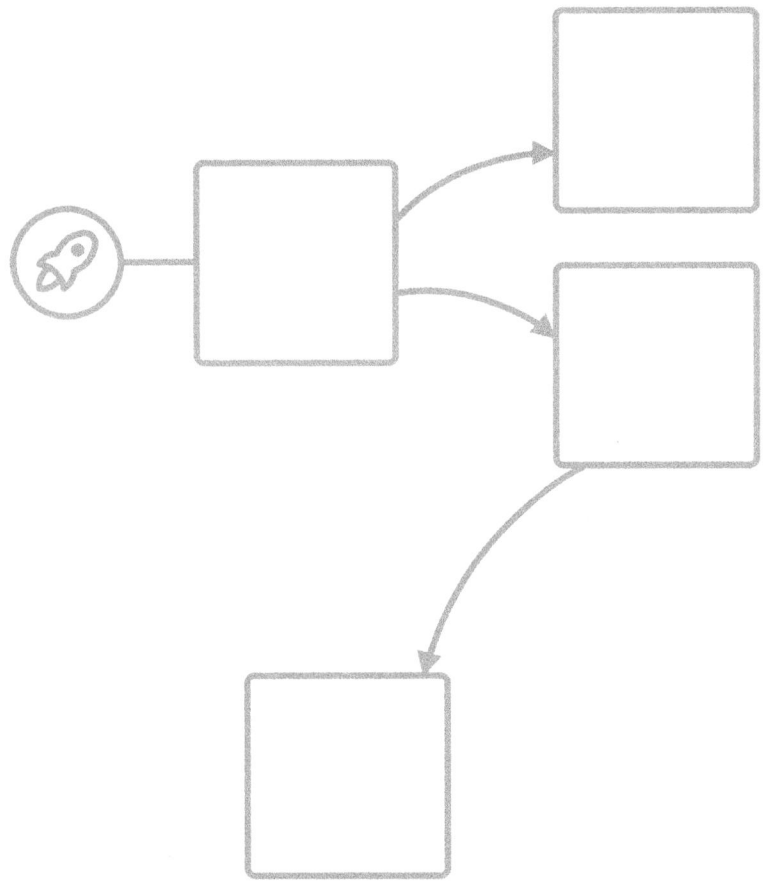

Reviewing HTML

HyperText Markup Language (HTML) describes the structure of a document. The language has a series of *elements* that "markup" content to define how it is presented and arranged.

Elements

HTML documents start with a **<html>** element. It has an *opening tag* and *closing tag*.

```
<html></html>
```

An *opening tag* begins with a less-than sign, **<**, the name of the element, and greater-than sign, **>**. Following the opening tag is any content that is part of the element. It ends with a closing tag, a less-than sign, **<**, a backslash, **/**, the name of the element, and a greater-than sign, **>**.

- **Opening Tag: <html>**
- **Content:**
- **Closing Tag </html>**

Elements exist in connection to each other in a parent and child relationship.

```
<html>
  <body></body>
</html>
```

If one or more elements are content inside an element, it is their *parent*.

- **Parent: <html>**
- **Children: <body>**

Head and Body

HTML documents start with **<html>**. This element has two children: **<head>** and **<body>**.

Head

The **<head>** element contains information about the document such as its title, author, and other details about the document.

```
<html>
  <head>
    <title>Example Document!</title>
  </head>
</html>
```

Body

The **<body>** element contains the content of a document. Anything that is part of the document and not a child of the **<head>** will be in the **<body>** element.

```
<html>
  <body></body>
</html>
```

Common HTML Elements

The most current version of HTML allows for new elements to be added and used in a document without issue. However, there are many common HTML elements defined in earlier versions and frequently used to structure documents.

- **<p>**: Paragraph element, **<p>**, is most commonly used to store large groups of text.
- **<strong>**: Strong emphasis, **<strong>**, gives a **strong emphasis** to its content.
- **<em>**: Emphasis, **<em>**, gives an *emphasis* to its content.
- **<div>**: Division, **<div>**, "divides" up a document. It is very common to use **<div>** elements to logically separate content in a larger document.
- **<a>**: Anchor element. Hyperlinks are created through using *anchors*, **<a>**.

Attributes

All elements have access to *attributes*. Inside of the opening tag of an element, values can be used to configure or adjust how the element is displayed or understood.

Attributes are written in a **property="value"** format where the *property* is assigned a "value" inside of quotation marks.

```
<a href="https://www.google.com/">Link to Google</a>
```

The most common attribute is *href* (hyper-reference) as used with **<a>**. It defines what the hyperlink links to from the anchor. However, there is a large number of possible attributes.

id

All elements can use the **id** attribute. It should be a unique value within the document. It's an *identification*.

```
<div id="example">
Content
</div>
```

When working with CSS, using the **id** attribute also allows its unique value to be "selected" and styled in certain ways.

class

All elements can use the **class** attribute. It can be a repeating value within the document. It's a *classification* that can be used across multiple elements.

```
<div class="example">
Content
</div>
```

When working with CSS, using the **class** attribute also allows its value to be used multiple times.

Using HTML in Twine

HTML elements like **<p>** can be used inside of passages in Twine. In fact, all story formats support using elements to better structure content.

Chapbook HTML

Chapbook uses a variety of HTML elements and attributes to organize its stories. The following is a snapshot of a Chapbook story for reference and archival purposes.

```html
<form id="cb-validation" action="javascript:void(0)">
  <button id="cb-validation-tester" hidden=""></button>
  <button id="cb-block-enter-key" hidden=""></button>
  <div id="backdrop">
    <div id="page" aria-live="polite">
      <header>
        <div class="left"></div>
        <div class="center"></div>
        <div class="right"></div>
      </header>
      <article style="position: relative;">
        <div class="" style="">
          <p>Double-click this passage to edit it.</p>
        </div>
      </article>
      <ul class="warnings" hidden=""></ul>
      <footer class="has-content">
        <div class="left">
          <p>
            <em>Chapbook HTML</em>
          </p>
        </div>
        <div class="center"></div>
        <div class="right">
          <p>
           <a href="javascript:void(0)" data-cb-restart="true">Restart</a>
          </p>
        </div>
      </footer>
      <div id="spinner">
        <img src="data:image/svg+xml..." width="40" height="40" alt="">
      </div>
```

```
    </div>
  </div>
</form>
```

Harlowe HTML

Harlowe uses a variety of HTML elements and attributes to organize its stories.

The following are snapshots of HTML element differences between major versions in Harlowe.

Harlowe 1.X

```
<tw-story>
  <tw-passage>
    <tw-sidebar>
    <tw-icon tabindex="0" class="undo" title="Undo" style="visibility: hidden;"> </tw-icon>
    <tw-icon tabindex="0" class="redo" title="Redo" style="visibility: hidden;"> </tw-icon>
    </tw-sidebar>
    <tw-expression type="macro" name="link-goto">
      <tw-link tabindex="0" passage-name="Another" data-raw="">Another</tw-link>
    </tw-expression>
  </tw-passage>
</tw-story>
```

Harlowe 2.X

```
<tw-story tags="">
  <tw-passage tags="">
  <tw-sidebar>
    <tw-icon tabindex="0" class="undo" title="Undo" style="visibility: hidden;"> </tw-icon>
    <tw-icon tabindex="0" class="redo" title="Redo" style="visibility: hidden;"> </tw-icon>
  </tw-sidebar>
  <tw-expression type="macro" name="link-goto">
    <tw-link tabindex="0" passage-name="Another" data-raw="">Another</tw-link>
  </tw-expression>
  </tw-passage>
</tw-story>
```

Harlowe 3.X

```
<tw-story tags="">
  <tw-passage tags="">
    <tw-sidebar>
       <tw-icon tabindex="0" class="undo" title="Undo" style="visibility: hidden;">↶</tw-icon>
       <tw-icon tabindex="0" class="redo" title="Redo" style="visibility: hidden;">↷</tw-icon>
    </tw-sidebar>
    <tw-expression type="macro" name="link-goto">
      <tw-link tabindex="0" data-raw="">Another</tw-link>
    </tw-expression>
  </tw-passage>
</tw-story>
```

SugarCube HTML

SugarCube uses a variety of HTML elements and attributes to organize its stories.

The following are snapshots of HTML element differences between major versions in SugarCube.

SugarCube 1.X

```html
<body>
  <div id="init-screen">
    <p id="init-loading">Initializing. Please wait…<br><progress></progress></p>
  </div>
  <div id="ui-bar">
    <header id="title" role="banner">
      <div id="story-banner"></div>
      <h1 id="story-title">SugarCube HTML</h1>
      <div id="story-subtitle"></div>
      <div id="story-title-separator"></div>
      <p id="story-author"></p>
    </header>
    <nav id="menu" role="navigation">
      <ul id="menu-core">
        <li id="menu-saves"><a>Saves</a></li>
        <li id="menu-restart"><a>Restart</a></li>
      </ul>
    </nav>
  </div>
  <div id="passages" role="main">
    <section id="passage-untitled-passage" class="passage" data-passage="Untitled Passage" style="visibility: visible;">
      <header class="header"></header>
      <div class="body content">Double-click this passage to edit it.</div>
      <footer class="footer"></footer>
    </section>
  </div>
```

```
    <div id="ui-overlay" class="ui-close"></div>
    <div id="ui-body"></div>
    <a id="ui-body-close" class="ui-close"> </a>
    ...
</body>
```

SugarCube 2.X

```
<body>
  <div id="init-screen">
    <div id="init-loading">
      <div>Loading…</div>
    </div>
  </div>
  ...
  <div id="ui-overlay" class="ui-close"></div>
  <div id="ui-dialog" tabindex="0" role="dialog" aria-labelledby="ui-dialog-title">
    <div id="ui-dialog-titlebar">
      <h1 id="ui-dialog-title"></h1>
      <button id="ui-dialog-close" class="ui-close" tabindex="0" aria-label="Close"> </button>
    </div>
    <div id="ui-dialog-body"></div>
  </div>
  <div id="ui-bar">
    <div id="ui-bar-tray">
      <button id="ui-bar-toggle" tabindex="0" title="Toggle the UI bar" aria-label="Toggle the UI bar" type="button"></button>
        <div id="ui-bar-history">
          <button id="history-backward" tabindex="0" title="Go backward within the game history" aria-label="Go backward within the game history" disabled="" aria-disabled="true" type="button"> </button>
          <button id="history-forward" tabindex="0" title="Go forward within the game history" aria-label="Go forward within the game history" disabled="" aria-disabled="true" type="button"> </button>
        </div>
    </div>
    <div id="ui-bar-body">
```

```
      <header id="title" role="banner">
        <div id="story-banner"></div>
        <h1 id="story-title">SugarCube HTML</h1>
        <div id="story-subtitle"></div>
        <div id="story-title-separator"></div>
        <p id="story-author"></p>
      </header>
      <nav id="menu" role="navigation">
        <ul id="menu-core">
          <li id="menu-item-saves">
            <a tabindex="0">Saves</a>
          </li>
          <li id="menu-item-restart">
            <a tabindex="0">Restart</a>
          </li>
        </ul>
      </nav>
    </div>
  </div>
  <div id="story" role="main">
    <div id="passages">
      <div id="passage-untitled-passage" data-passage="Untitled Passage" class="passage">Double-click this passage to edit it.</div>
    </div>
  </div>
  ...
</body>
```

Snowman HTML

Snowman uses a variety of HTML elements and attributes to organize its stories.

The following are snapshots of HTML element differences between major versions in Snowman.

Snowman 1.X

```
<body>
  <div id="main">
    <div class="passage" aria-live="polite">
      <p>Double-click this passage to edit it.</p>
    </div>
  </div>
</body>
```

Snowman 2.X

```
<body>
  <tw-story>
    <tw-passage class="passage" aria-live="polite">
      <p>Double-click this passage to edit it.</p>
    </tw-passage>
  </tw-story>
</body>
```

Working with CSS

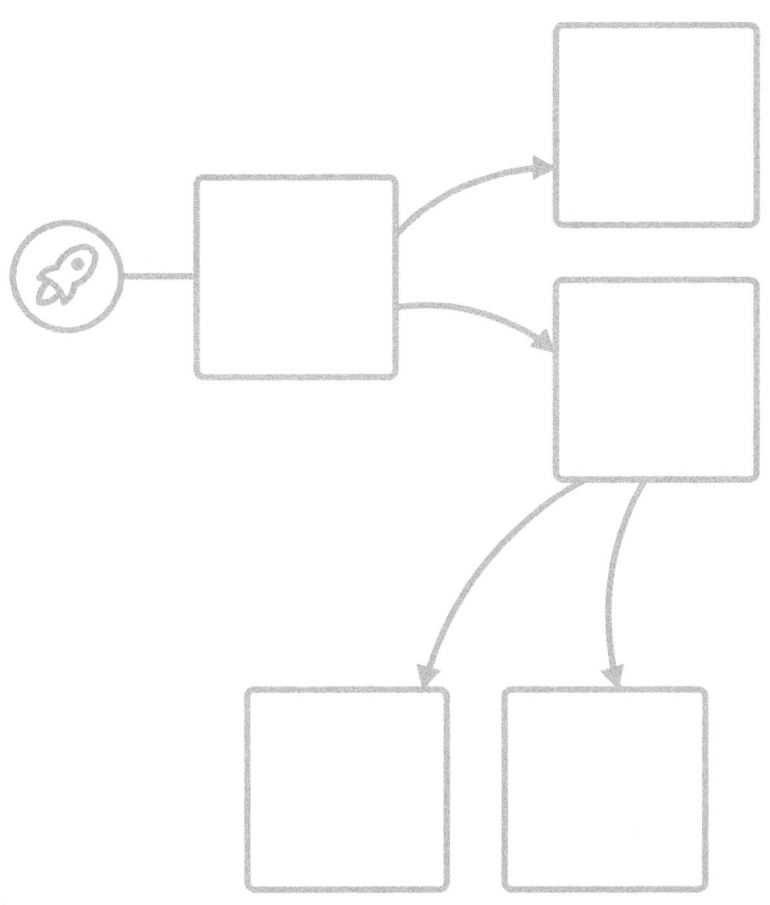

Reviewing CSS Selectors

Cascading StyleSheets (CSS) is a programming language for defining the presentation of HyperText Markup Language (HTML). Stylesheets "cascade" because values are passed from parent HTML elements to their children.

Declarations

Declarations are written as a series of *properties* and *values*. Each has a property, colon (:), value, and end with a semicolon, ;.

They "declare" the property has a certain value.

```
color: red;
```

Declaration Blocks

CSS is written in groups of declarations called *blocks*.

```
{
  color: red;
  background: blue;
}
```

A *declaration block* begins with an opening curly bracket and ends with a closing curly bracket.

Selectors

In order to apply the declarations to content, a *selector* is needed. This "selects" where in the document to apply the declarations.

There are many different possible selector combinations. Three of the most common are type, class, and ID.

Type

A *type* selector finds one or more elements based on their name.

CSS:

```
p {
  color: red;
}
```

HTML:

```
<p>This would be red!</p>
```

Class

A *class* selector finds one or more elements on their **class** attribute. Class selectors starts with a period, ..

CSS:

```
.redFont {
  color: red;
}
```

HTML:

```
<p class="redFont">This would be red!</p>
```

ID

An *ID* selector finds one or more elements based on their **id** attribute. ID selectors start with a hash, **#**.

CSS:

```
#redFont {
  color: red;
}
```

HTML:

```
<p id="redFont">This would be red!</p>
```

Ruleset

A *ruleset* is a combination of one or more selectors with a declaration block. They are often simply called "rules" or "CSS rules" when referring to them as groups.

CSS:

```
body {
   font-size: 1.2em;
}
#redFont {
   color: red;
}
```

HTML:

```
<body>
   <div id="redFont">This would be larger and in red!</div>
</body>
```

Chapbook CSS

Stories in Chapbook can be styled in different ways through using its Vars Section.

Chapbook defines the global object **config.style** for changing these.

Fonts and Colors

Fonts and colors can be adjusted in Chapbook through using the objects of **header, page**, and **footer** areas as part of the global **config.style**.

Example:

```
config.style.page.color: "red-6"
--

Passage content
```

Note: Chapbook uses a specific syntax for writing colors using the Open Colors system.

Header and Footer

Passage content in Chapbook is also divided into seven areas in the following arrangement.

config.header.left	config.header.center	config.header.right
	main passage text	
config.footer.left	config.footer.center	config.footer.right

These correspond to elements with different classes (left, center, right) for both **<header>** and **<footer>**. Passage content is stored in an **<article>** element.

```
<div id="page" aria-live="polite">
  <header>
    <div class="left"></div>
    <div class="center"></div>
    <div class="right"></div>
  </header>
  <article style="position: relative;">
    <div class="" style="">
      <p>Double-click this passage to edit it.</p>
    </div>
  </article>
    <footer class="has-content">
      <div class="left"></div>
      <div class="center"></div>
      <div class="right"></div>
    </footer>
</div>
```

Overwriting Chapbook CSS

Warning
Overwriting existing CSS rules is an *advanced* technique. It has the potential to significantly change the presentation of content.

All Chapbook stories follow the same HTML structure.

Page > Article

All passage content is shown to users as part of an element with the *id* of **page** with an `<article>` element.

```
<div id="page" aria-live="polite">
  <article style="position: relative;">
    <div class="" style="">
      <p>Double-click this passage to edit it.</p>
    </div>
  </article>
</div>
```

Targeting this selector allows for changing the presentation of passage content.

Example CSS:

```
#page article {
  background-color: black;
  color: purple;
}
```

Page > A

Passage links are represented as **<a>** elements in Chapbook.

Using the selector of **#page a** allows for changing the presentation of links in a story.

Example CSS:

```
#page a {
  color: purple;
  border: 2px solid red;
}
```

Harlowe CSS

Harlowe strongly encourages authors to style stories through using macros and named hooks.

Named Hooks

Page

?Page: Affects the `<tw-story>` element.

Example:

```
(enchant: ?Page, (text-color: yellow) + (text-style:'bold'))
Yellow text in a bold style!
```

Passage

?Passage: Affects the `<tw-passage>` element), allowing **(text-colour:)**, **(font:)**, or **(css:)** usage with text content.

Example:

```
(enchant: ?Passage, (text-color: green) + (background: red))
Red background and green text!
```

Sidebar

?Sidebar: Affects the `<tw-sidebar>` element, allowing macros like **(replace:)** or **(append:)** to change text content.

Example:

```
(replace: ?Sidebar)[This is the new sidebar content!]

[[Another Passage]]
```

Link

?Link: Affects all of the links (passage links and **(link:)**) in the passage.

Example:

```
(enchant: ?Link, (color: green) )

[[Not blue, only green]]
```

Overwriting Harlowe CSS

> **Warning**
> Overwriting existing CSS rules is an *advanced* technique. It has the potential to significantly change the presentation of content.

All Harlowe stories follow the same HTML structure.

tw-passage

Like working with **?Passage**, using the type selector with **tw-passage** allows for overriding or augmenting the existing declarations.

```
tw-passage { /* Your CSS Here */ }
```

tw-link

When creating hyperlinks, Harlowe uses the **<tw-link>** element.

```
tw-link {/* Your CSS Here */ }
```

SugarCube CSS

> **Warning**
> Overwriting existing CSS rules is an *advanced* technique. It has the potential to significantly change the presentation of content.

All SugarCube stories follow the same HTML structure.

The SugarCube documentation has extensive details on the selectors available in the story format.

Overwriting SugarCube CSS

SugarCube Passage

```
.passage { /* Your CSS Here */ }
```

SugarCube Links

SugarCube uses the anchor element, **<a>**, to create hyperlinks.

```
.passage a {   /* Your CSS Here */ }
.passage a:hover {   /* Your CSS Here */ }
.passage a:active {   /* Your CSS Here */ }
```

Passage Names

All passages are given the *id* attribute value as their name with the prefix of **passage-**.

Any with spaces between words or characters are converted into hyphens. All letters are converted into lowercase.

Example:

```
#passage-untitled-passage { /* Your CSS Here */ }
```

If a passage is included via the **<<include>>** macro, its name is added to the class list for the passage element. It can be used as a class selector instead.

Example:

```
.passage-additional-passage { /* Your CSS Here */ }
```

Snowman CSS

> **Warning**
> Overwriting existing CSS rules is an *advanced* technique. It has the potential to significantly change the presentation of content.

Snowman 1.X provides a limited set of CSS selectors and declarations.

Snowman 1.X

```
body {
  font: 18px "Helvetica Neue", Helvetica, Arial, sans-serif;
  color: #222;
}

#main {
  max-width: 38em;
  margin: 0 auto;
  line-height: 145%;
}

a {
  color: #222;
  text-decoration-color: #bbb;
}

a:hover {
  color: #cc8929;
  text-decoration-color: #cc8929;
}

a:active {
  color: #ffb040;
  text-decoration-color: #cc8929;
}
```

Snowman 2.X

Snowman 2.X includes normalize.css with its existing CSS code.

```css
body {
  font: 1.5em "Helvetica Neue", Helvetica, Arial, sans-serif;
  color: #222;
  margin: 0.5em;
}

tw-story {
  max-width: 35em;
  margin: 0 auto;
  line-height: 150%;
  display: block;
}

tw-passage {
  display: block;
}

a {
  color: #222;
  text-decoration-color: #ccc;
}

a:hover {
  color: #cc8929;
  text-decoration-color: #cc8929;
}

a:active {
  color: #ffb040;
  text-decoration-color: #cc8929;
}
```

Snowman Links

Snowman uses the anchor element, **<a>**, for all links. However, as links are re-generated at the start of each passage, the pseudo-class `visited` will not have an effect. **hover**, however, will.

```
a {
  color: blue;
}

a:hover {
  color: green;
}
```

Overwriting CSS

Snowman 1.X Passage

```
#main { /* Your CSS Here */ }
```

Snowman 2.X Passage

```
tw-passage { /* Your CSS Here */ }
```

Working with JavaScript

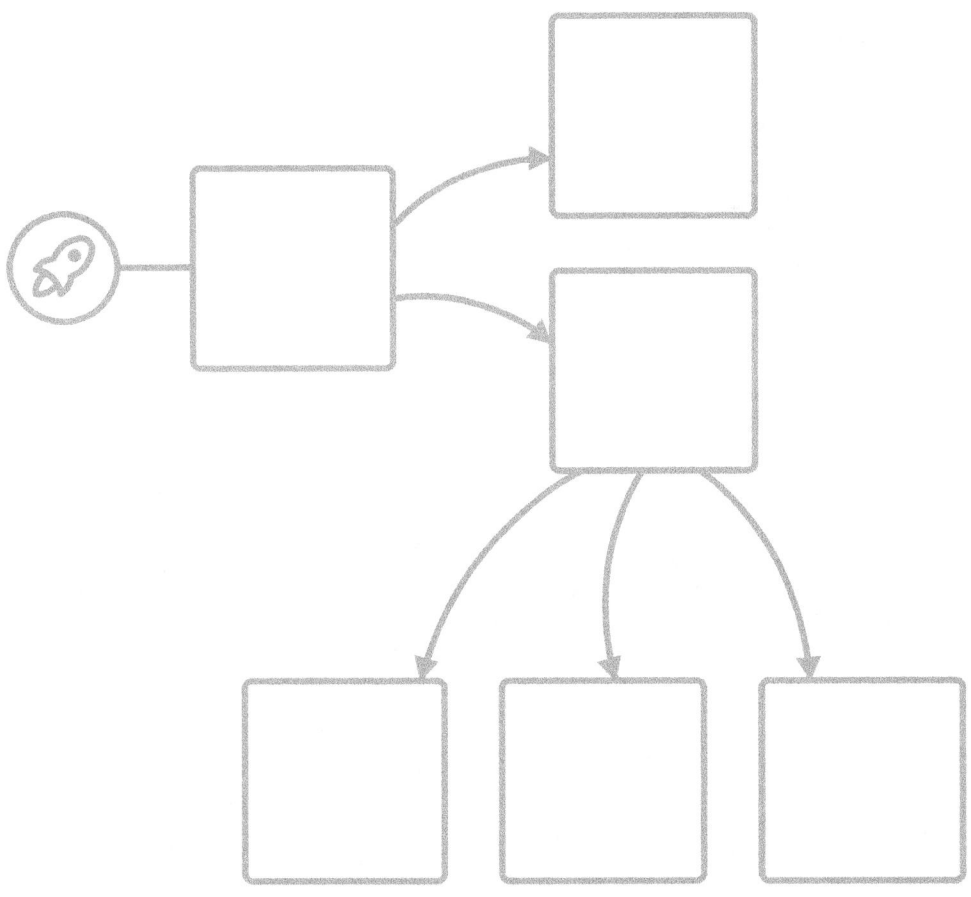

Reviewing JavaScript

JavaScript is a programming language available in web browsers. It allows developers to write code that runs when a hypertext document is shown to a user in a web browser.

Script Element

JavaScript code appears in the `<script>` element in HTML.

Document Object Model (DOM)

Web browsers provide all JavaScript code with a global object named **document**. This represents the entire HTML document as an **object** with properties and method for manipulating its content. This allows code to read and change the document while it is shown to a user in a web browser.

Story Formats Are JavaScript

Twine records the contents of a story as HTML. This is read and processed by a story format written in JavaScript.

Publishing a HTML file with Twine means bundling the story format *and* story content together in one file.

Story JavaScript

Every story has access to its Story JavaScript.

Any JavaScript code added to Story JavaScript will be run *before* any content of a story.

This is a useful space for adding more JavaScript code to a story or preparing values to be used before a story is run.

Chapbook JavaScript

Chapbook enables JavaScript support through its **[JavaScript]** modifier.

Accessing Variables

Variables are normally accessed and their values changed through the Vars Section of a passages.

Chapbook also provides the global object **engine.state** and its methods **set(variable, value)** and **get(variable)** for accessing story variables.

> **Reminder:** A *story variable* is one which exists for as long as the story is running.
>
> In Chapbook, they are defined in the Vars Section and remain until the story stops.

State Set

The method **engine.state.set()** will either update a variable's value, if it exists, or create the variable, if it does not. (The name of the variable should be enclosed in quotation marks.)

```
[JavaScript]
engine.state.set('example', 'Hi!');
[continued]

{example}
```

State Get

The method **engine.state.get()** will retrieve the value of a variable. If it does not exist, the value returned will be **undefined**.

```
example: "Hi!"
--

[JavaScript]
let example = engine.state.get('example');
write(example);
```

Writing Values

Chapbook provides the function **write()** for adding values to the content of a passage inside of the **[JavaScript]** modifier.

```
Jolene,

Jolene,

[JavaScript]
write("Jolene,");
[continued]

Jolene.
```

Harlowe JavaScript

Harlowe provides many macros for editing how content is displayed or used in a story.

The Harlowe documentation purposely does not include instructions for editing or changing the JavaScript code or related values used in the story format.

It is *strongly recommended* to not change the JavaScript code or any of its values in Harlowe.

SugarCube JavaScript

The SugarCube documentation provides details for using Scripting Macros with JavaScript code. It also provides multiple application programming interfaces (APIs) for using JavaScript with its own built-in functionality.

`windows.setup`

When working with Story JavaScript, it is strongly recommended, to use the **setup** object in SugarCube to add functionality.

```
window.setup = window.setup || {};
```

SugarCube Addons

Working with SugarCube Addons requires using Story JavaScript. The provided instructions with the addon often require copying and pasting code into this area or configuring other options.

Snowman JavaScript

Snowman does not come with any macros, but it does bundle the libraries of Underscore, JQuery, and Marked.

Working with Templates

Because Snowman comes with Underscore, it supports writing JavaScript in passages using its template system.

Arbitrary Code

The opening **<%** and closing **%>** template tags allow for writing arbitrary JavaScript in a passage.

```
<%
 let example = "Hi!";
 print(example);
%>
```

Interpolating

The use of the opening **<%=** tag for templates *interpolates* any values it encounters. In other words, it is an easy way to include JavaScript values in passages.

```
I've made mistakes, Lord struck me down

<%= "Caught in a landslide, lost underground" %>

I hear them gates, swing open wide

<%= "Come close to midnight, hell fade me down" %>
```

print()

Underscore provides the function **print()** inside of any template code. This can be used to "print" values from inside an arbitrary code template block.

```
Running from the violence

<%
  print("(Oh, oh. ");
  print("Oh, oh)");
%>

Running from the violence
```

Global s

Inside any use of templates tags also have access to the global variable **s**. This is a short-hand for **window.story.state**, and it can be used to create the effect of story variables through creating global properties in JavaScript.

> **Note:** Any variables created in a code block or in a **<script>** element in Snowman are *local* to that scope. The only way to share values across passages is through global objects like **s**.

```
:: Untiled Passage
<%
  s.example = "Hi!";
%>

[[Another]]

:: Another
<%= s.example %>
```

Twine 2 Examples

Chapbook

Adding Functionality

Summary

Chapbook allows for creation of custom inserts and modifiers.

The example below adds an insert that displays a 😃 emoji.

Twee Code

```
:: StoryTitle
Adding Functionality

:: UserScript[script]
engine.extend('1.0.0', () => {
    config.template.inserts = [{
        match: /^smiley face$/i,
        render: () => '😃'
    }, ...config.template.inserts];
});

:: Start
Hello there {smiley face}
```

Arrays

Summary

Using the Vars Section, variables can be set using any JavaScript values, such as arrays. However, Chapbook expressions cannot show an array or its value by position. However, a new variable can be set using values from the array and then shown. This following example shows how to take this approach.

Twee Code

```
:: StoryTitle
Arrays for Chapbook

:: Start
arrayExample: [13, 15]
exampleValue: arrayExample[0]
--
Chapbook can't display indexed array values currently. However, setting a value based on a position in an array will show.

Here is an {exampleValue}.
```

Audio

> **Information**
> This examples uses two additional files, **testpattern.ogg** and **testpattern.wav**. Both files need to be downloaded from the online Cookbook and placed in the same folder as the HTML file in order to work as designed.

Summary

Chapbook supports both looping sounds (which it calls ambient) and one-off sound (which it calls effects). It only allows playing one sound at a time.

Twee Code

```
:: Start
sound.ambient.test.url: 'testpattern.ogg'
sound.ambient.test.description: 'An audio test pattern'
--

> [[Play sound]]
> [[Stop the sound]]

:: Play sound
{ambient sound: 'test'}

[[Return->Start]]

:: Stop the sound
sound.ambient.test.playing: false
--

[[Return->Start]]
```

Chapbook: Setting and Showing Variables (pg. 108)

CSS and Passage Tags

Summary

Using the built-in global variable *config*, text colors and other CSS properties can be programmatically adjusted using the **[JavaScript]** modifier in Chapbook.

Twee Code

```
:: StoryTitle
Chapbook: CSS and Passage Tags

:: Start
config.style.page.color: "yellow-4"
--
This is one color!
[JavaScript]
// Overwrite the default text color
config.style.page.color = "violet-6";
[continued]

And this is the same color!
```

Cycling Choices

Summary

Chapbook provides the **{cycling link}** modifier for creating a cycling link effect.

Twee Code

```
:: StoryTitle
Chapbook: Cycling Links

:: Start
This cycling link example remembers the choice made:
{cycling link for: 'hair', choices: ["Black", "Brown", "Blonde", "Red", "White"]}

This cycling-link example will disappear (show empty string) on its last choice:
{cycling link for: 'breakfast', choices: ["Two eggs", "One egg", ""]}
```

Date and Time

Summary

Using lookups, Chapbook can easily retrieve the current month, day, and year.

Twee Code

```
:: StoryTitle
Date and Time in Chapbook

:: Start
The current month number is {now.month}.

The current day number is {now.day}.

The current full-year number is {now.year}.
```

Delayed Text

Summary

In Chapbook, the **[after]** modifier shows text after a set amount of time.

Twee Code

```
:: StoryTitle
Chapbook: Delayed Text

:: Start
[after 5s; append]
It has been 5 seconds. Show the text!
```

Deleting Variables

Summary

While variables created using the **[JavaScript]** modifier can be deleted within their blocks, any created within the Vars Section can simply be set to **undefined** to make them unable to be shown within an expression by using the **engine.state.set()** function.

Twee Code

```
:: StoryTitle
Chapbook: Deleting Variables

:: Start
color: "red"
--
[JavaScript]
engine.state.set("color", undefined)
[continued]
What is color? {color}
```

Dice Rolling

Summary

This example demonstrates how to create the same effects of rolling various physical dice through using the *random* global variable in Chapbook.

Inserts are used to display the use of *random* in the passage. For calculations, a var section and temporary variables are used because expressions cannot be used within inserts.

Twee Code

```
:: StoryTitle
Chapbook: Rolling Dice

:: Start
_example1: random.d4 + 4
_example2: random.d6 - 2
_example3: random.d6 + random.d6 + 10
--

Rolling a 1d4: {random.d4}

Rolling a 1d6: {random.d6}

Rolling a 1d8: {random.d8}

Rolling a 1d10: {random.d10}

Rolling a 1d12: {random.d12}

Rolling a 1d20: {random.d20}

Rolling a 1d100: {random.d100}
```

Dropdown

Summary

The insert **{dropdown}** is used to create a dropdown menu in Chapbook. The **for:** option specifies where to save the selected value and the **choices:** option defines what the choices should be for the user.

Twee Code

```
:: StoryTitle
Chapbook: Dropdown

:: Start
{dropdown menu for: "chosenValue", choices: ["Up", "Down", "Left", "Right"]}

[[Check Choice]]

:: Check Choice
You chose {chosenValue}.
```

Fairmath System

Summary

"Fairmath System" demonstrates how to re-create the Fairmath system found in ChoiceScript. Based on the operation, increasing and decreasing changes the value by a percentage as the difference between the original and adjusted value.

This example defines functions in the Story JavaScript, which are then used in the Vars Section of a passage to set values. These are shown using expressions within the text of the passage itself.

Twee Code

```
:: StoryTitle
Chapbook: Fairmath

:: UserScript[script]
// Create a global object
window.setup = window.setup || {};

// Create a fairmath global object
window.setup.fairmath = {};

// Create an 'increase' function
setup.fairmath.increase = function(x,y) {
    return Math.round(x+((100-x)*(y/100)));
};

// Create a "decrease" function
setup.fairmath.decrease = function(x,y) {
    return Math.round(x-(x*(y/100)));
};

:: Start
```

```
decreaseExample: setup.fairmath.decrease(100, 50)
increaseExample: setup.fairmath.increase(50, 50)
--
```

Decrease 100 by 50% using Fairmath:
Decrease Example: {decreaseExample}

Increase 50 by 50% using Fairmath:
Increase Example: {increaseExample}

Geolocation

Summary

Many browsers allow access to the user's current location through the Geolocation property and associated functions. This functionality is subject to the user agreeing to allow access. Until the functionality is unlocked, or if the user declines, default values will be returned.

Functionality availability and their results should always be tested against other location services or information. Most browsers will return results through the fastest and sometimes least-accurate methods possible.

In this example, the **[JavaScript]** modifier is used to test for, run, and show data using an **alert()** from the JavaScript functions.

Twee Code

```
:: StoryTitle
Chapbook: Geolocation

:: UserScript[script]
(function () {

  window.geolocation = {

    available: function() {
      return ("geolocation" in navigator
        && typeof navigator.geolocation.getCurrentPosition === "function");
    },
    getLocation: function() {

      // Create initial values
      var location = { latitude : 0, longitude : 0 };

      // Create success callback to store values
```

```
    var  positionSuccess = function (position) {

      location.latitude = position.coords.latitude;
      location.longitude = position.coords.longitude;

    };

    // Create error callback
    var positionError = function (error) {
      /* Code that handles errors */
    };

    // Create initial options
    var positionOptions = {
      timeout: 31000,
      enableHighAccuracy: true,
      maximumAge : 120000
    };


    // Ask for location based on callbacks and options
    navigator.geolocation.getCurrentPosition(
      positionSuccess,
      positionError,
      positionOptions
    );

    // Return location found
    // If not location, will return initial (0,0) values
    return location;

  },
  approximateLocation: function (a, b, allowedDiff) {
      // allowedDiff must always be > 0
    if (a === b) { // handles various "exact" edge cases
      return true;
    }

    allowedDiff = allowedDiff || 0.0005;
```

```
        return Math.abs(a - b) < allowedDiff;
    }

  };

}());

:: Start
[[GeoLocation]]

:: GeoLocation
[JavaScript]
if(window.geolocation.available() ) {
    var geolocation = window.geolocation.getLocation();
  alert("Latitude: " + geolocation.latitude + " Longitude:" + geolocation.longitude);
}
[continued]
```

Google Fonts

Summary

Chapbook provides a global variable, *config.style.googleFont*, that can be used within the Vars Section to load and use an external font.

Twee Code

```
:: StoryTitle
Chapbook: Google Fonts

:: Start
config.style.googleFont: '<link href="https://fonts.googleapis.com/css?family=Roboto" rel="stylesheet">'
config.style.page.font: 'Roboto'
--
This text is styled by a Google Font.
```

Headers and Footers

Summary

Chapbook provides two global variables, *config.header* and *config.footer*, that each have the properties *left*, *right*, and *center*. When set, these properties show their content as the header or footer in the particular position matching its property name.

Twee Code

```
:: StoryTitle
Chapbook: Header and Footer

:: Start
config.header.center: "This is the header!"
config.footer.center: "This is the footer!"
--
This is content.
```

Images

Summary

When using Chapbook, images can be displayed through the image HTML element and **url()** CSS data type when encoded as Base64.

When using an image element, its source is either absolutely or relatively located. An absolute reference starts with HTTP or another protocol; a relative reference describes the location of the image in relation to the webpage.

Because images are external resources, they need to be included with the webpage as Base64-encoded or in another location. While Base64-encoded images can be embedded in a webpage, it also increases its overall size. External images require additional hosting and are included through their reference in CSS (URL) data type or image (SRC) attribute.

Twee Code

```
:: StoryTitle
Images in Chapbook

:: UserStylesheet[stylesheet]
.base64image {
  width: 256px;
  height: 256px;
  /* Base64 image truncated for example */
  /* See Twee file for full version. */
  background-image: url('data:image/png;base64...');
}

:: Start
This is an image element:

<img src="https://twinery.org/homepage/img/logo.svg" width="256" height="256">
```

This is a base-64-encoded CSS image background:

<div class="base64image"></div>

Importing External JavaScript

> **Information**
> This example uses code from Three.js, a library for creating 3D graphics in the browser. It is include only for demonstrational purposes and its own documentation should be consulted to understand its functionality.

Summary

To include external JavaScript, it must first be loaded. This example uses code from the Mozilla Developer Network to dynamically import scripts. The example library loaded is Three.js.

Once loaded, a callback function is used to create a simple Three.js example and, if the browser supports it, shows a rotating 3D cube within the passage.

Twee Code

```
:: StoryTitle
Chapbook: Importing External JS

:: UserScript[script]
// The following code is used from MDN for
// dynamically importing scripts
// https://developer.mozilla.org/en-US/docs/Web/API/HTMLScriptElement#Dynamically_importing_scripts

window.setup = {};

setup.loadError = function(oError) {
  throw new URIError("The script " + oError.target.src + " didn't load correctly.");
};
```

```
setup.loadScript = function(url, onloadFunction) {
  var newScript = document.createElement("script");
  newScript.onerror = setup.loadError;
  if (onloadFunction) { newScript.onload = onloadFunction; }
  document.head.appendChild(newScript);
  newScript.async = true;
  newScript.src = url;
};


:: Start
<div id="drawArea"></div>
[JavaScript]
setup.loadScript("https://ajax.googleapis.com/ajax/libs/threejs/r84/three.min.js",
function() {
  var scene = new THREE.Scene();
  var camera = new THREE.PerspectiveCamera(
    75,
    1,
    0.1,
    1000 );

  var renderer = new THREE.WebGLRenderer();
  renderer.setSize( 250, 250 );
  document.getElementById("drawArea").appendChild( renderer.domElement );

  var geometry = new THREE.BoxGeometry( 1, 1, 1 );
  var material = new THREE.MeshBasicMaterial( { color: 0x00ff00 } );
  var cube = new THREE.Mesh( geometry, material );
  scene.add( cube );

  camera.position.z = 5;

  var animate = function () {
    requestAnimationFrame( animate );

    cube.rotation.x += 0.01;
    cube.rotation.y += 0.01;
```

```
    renderer.render( scene, camera );
  };

  animate();

});
```

[continued]

Keyboard Events

Summary

"Keyboard Events" demonstrates how to capture keyboard events and then how to associate individual keys with activities within a story.

The example uses **addEventListener()** to monitor for all "keyup" events. Once a "keyup" event has occurred, two values are available:

- The *keyCode* property: the numerical value representing the key presented in its decimal ASCII code supported by effectively all browsers.
- The *key* property: the string value of the key presented supported by most modern web-browsers.

Twee Code

```
:: StoryTitle
Chapbook: Keyboard

:: UserScript[script]
(function () {
  document.addEventListener('keyup', function (ev) {
    /* the ev variable contains a keyup event object.
     *
     * ev.keyCode - contains the ASCII code of the key that was released, this property is supported in effectively all browsers.
     * ev.key     - contains the key value of the key that was released, this property is supported by most modern browsers.
     *
     */

    /* the following shows an alert when the 'a' key is released. */
    if (ev.key === 'a') {
      alert("the 'a' key was released.");
```

```
    }
  });
}());
```

:: Start
Press and release the "a" key to show an Alert dialog.

Lock and Key: Variable

Summary

"Lock and Key: Variable" demonstrates how to create the effect of picking up a key and unlocking a door. In this example, the key is a variable (*key*) and is initially set to the value "false" in the Start passage.

When the link "Pick up key" is clicked in the "Back Room" passage, *key* is changed to the value "true" via embedding the passage "Key". When the passage is visited and *key* is set to the value of "true", door link changes from its initial response of "Locked Door" to "Unlock the door".

Twee Code

```
:: StoryTitle
Chapbook: Lock and Key: Variable

:: Start
key: false
--

Rooms:

[[Front Room]]

[[Back Room]]


:: Front Room
[if key == true]
  [[Unlock the door->Exit]]
[else]
  *Locked Door*
[continued]
```

Rooms:

[[Back Room]]

:: Back Room
[if key == false]
  Items:
  {reveal link: 'Pick up key', passage: 'Key'}
[else]
  There is nothing here.
[continued]

Rooms:

[[Front Room]]

:: Exit
You found the key and went through the door!

:: Key
key: true
--
You picked up the key!

Looping

Summary

In programming terminology, a "loop" is a common technique for iterating (moving through one by one) some type of data.

In Chapbook, the modifier **[JavaScript]** allows for using JavaScript inside a passage. Through using the **forEach()** function of Arrays and the **write()** function supplied by Chapbook, each entry within an array can be shown.

Twee Code

```
:: StoryTitle
Chapbook: Looping

:: Start
exampleArray: [2, 3, 5, 7, 11, 13, 17, 19, 23, 29, 31, 37, 41, 43, 47, 53, 59, 61]
--

The values of the array are:
<ul>
[JavaScript]
exampleArray.forEach(function(value, index){
  write("<li>" + value + "</li>");
});
[continued]
</ul>
```

Passages in Passages

Summary

Using the insert {embed passage: }, Chapbook can include one passage inside of another passage.

Twee Code

```
:: StoryTitle
Chapbook: Passages in Passages

:: Start
This is the Start passage!
{embed passage named: 'Another'}

:: Another
And this is another passage!
```

Passage Visits

Summary

In Chapbook, the lookup *passage.visits* variable contains the number of times the current passages has been visited by the user.

Twee Code

```
:: StoryTitle
Chapbook: Passage Visits

:: Start

[[Another Passage]]

:: Another Passage
How many times has the current passage been visited? {passage.visits}

[[Start]]
```

Player Statistics

Summary

Some of the most popular mechanics from table-top role-playing games are those where the player must determine their in-game statistics and then use them to make decisions.

In Chapbook, the values of variables can only be changed as part of the Vars Section or using JavaScript. This example combines the two and uses the **{embed passage}** modifier to use different passages as sections of code to adjust values based on user interactions.

Twee Code

```
:: StoryTitle
Chapbook: Player Statistics

:: Start
{embed passage: "Setup"}
{embed passage: "Statistics"}

:: IncreaseEmpathy
empathy: empathy + 1
points: points - 1
--
{embed passage: "Statistics"}

:: DecreaseEmpathy
empathy: empathy - 1
points: points + 1
--
{embed passage: "Statistics"}

:: IncreaseIntelligence
intelligence: intelligence + 1
points: points - 1
```

```
--
{embed passage: "Statistics"}

:: DecreaseIntelligence
intelligence: intelligence - 1
points: points + 1
--
{embed passage: "Statistics"}

:: Setup
empathy: 10
intelligence: 10
points: 5
--

:: Statistics
{embed passage: "CheckValues"}

[if points > 0 && empathy > 0]
Empathy:
[[[+]->IncreaseEmpathy]] [[[-]->DecreaseEmpathy]]
[continued]

[if points > 0 && intelligence > 0]
Intelligence:
[[[+]->IncreaseIntelligence]] [[[-]->DecreaseIntelligence]]
[continued]

Empathy: {empathy}

Intelligence: {intelligence}

Remaining Points: {points}

[[Reset Points->Start]]

:: CheckValues
[JavaScript]
    let empathy = engine.state.get('empathy');
```

```
let intelligence = engine.state.get('intelligence');
let points = engine.state.get('points');

if(empathy > 20){empathy = 20;}
if(intelligence > 20){intelligence = 20;}
if(points < 0){points = 0;}
if(points > 25){points = 25;}

engine.state.set('empathy', empathy);
engine.state.set('intelligence', intelligence);
engine.state.set('points', points);
```

Setting and Showing Variables

Summary

In Chapbook all variables are initialized and updated within the Vars Section of a passage. This section is always added at the beginning of the passage and there can only be one such section per passage. The Vars Section is separated from the passage's normal text by two dashes (--).

The value of a variable can be displayed using the **{insert}** insert.

Twee Code

```
:: StoryTitle
Setting and Showing Variables in Chapbook

:: Start
numberVariable: 5
wordVariable: "five"
phraseVariable: "The value"
--

{phraseVariable} is {numberVariable} and {wordVariable}.

{embed passage: "Increment number"}

The number variable was incremented by one to {numberVariable}.

:: Increment number
numberVariable: numberVariable + 1
--
```

Space Exploration

Summary

Games in the roguelike genre often have random events that influence player choices. Depending on these random events, a player's decisions can have lasting impact or even lead to the end of a session of play.

Heavily inspired by *FTL: Faster Than Light* (2012), this example generates a system of four planets consisting of either RED, more risk and more reward, or GREEN, less risk and less reward. Upon entering a system of planets, the player can choose to visit these planets and receive different events based on the outcome of a **Math.random()** function to select between several possible incidents. At the same time, the player must also balance the health of the ship, the number of jumps left, and the remaining fuel. These are all displayed when visiting the "Statistics" passage. If any of these statistics drop below 0, the game ends with a matching ending screen.

This example uses a complex combination of the Vars Section, **[JavaScript]** modifier, and internal JavaScript functionality in Chapbook, including the use of the function **window.go()**.

Twee Code

```
:: StoryTitle
Chapbook: Space Exploration

:: UserScript[script]
// Add a randomRange
// Used from https://developer.mozilla.org/en-US/docs/Web/JavaScript/Reference/Global_Objects/Math/random
Math.randomRange = (min, max) => {
    min = Math.ceil(min);
    max = Math.floor(max);
    return Math.floor(Math.random() * (max - min)) + min;
};
```

```
:: Start
health: 20
fuel: 4
system: []
numberOfJumpsLeft: 10
--
{embed passage: 'GenerateSystem'}

[[Explore Space]]

:: Explore Space
{embed passage: "CheckStatus"}
Current System:
{embed passage: 'DisplaySystem'}
<hr>
[[Hyperjump]]

[[Statistics]]

:: GenerateSystem
[JavaScript]

  // There will always be four (4) planets
  let planets = 4;

  // Reset global system
  let system = engine.state.get('system');
  system = [];

  // Add 0 (Red) or 1 (Green) planets
  for(let i = 0; i < planets; i++) {
    // Get a random number from 0 to 2
    // 0 = RED
    // 1 = GREEN
    // 2 = EMPTY
    system.push(Math.randomRange(0,3));
  }
```

```
  // Update the new 'system'
  engine.state.set('system', system);

:: CheckStatus
[JavaScript]
  let health = engine.state.get("health");
  let fuel = engine.state.get("fuel");
  let numberOfJumpsLeft = engine.state.get("numberOfJumpsLeft");

  if(health <= 0) {
    // Introduce a micro-delay before transition
    setTimeout(() => {
      go("Destroyed");
    }, 10);
  }

  if(fuel <= 0) {
    // Introduce a micro-delay before transition
    setTimeout(() => {
      go("Lost in Space");
    }, 10);
  }

  if(numberOfJumpsLeft <= 0) {
    // Introduce a micro-delay before transition
    setTimeout(() => {
      go("Safe");
    }, 10);
  }

:: Destroyed
The ship exploded in flight.

Game Over.

:: Lost in Space
Without fuel, the ship tumbled and spun in the endless black.

Game Over
```

:: Safe
After 10 hyperjumps, the ship left the hazardous area and called for help.

Success!

:: Hyperjump
fuel: fuel - 1
numberOfJumpsLeft: numberOfJumpsLeft - 1
--
{embed passage: "CheckStatus"}
{embed passage: "GenerateSystem"}

[[Scan System->Explore Space]]

:: DisplaySystem
[if system[0] == 0]
  {reveal link: 'RED', passage: 'RED'}
[if system[0] == 1]
  {reveal link: 'GREEN', passage: 'GREEN'}
[if system[0] == 2]

[if system[1] == 0]
  {reveal link: 'RED', passage: 'RED'}
[if system[1] == 1]
  {reveal link: 'GREEN', passage: 'GREEN'}
[if system[1] == 2]

[if system[2] == 0]
  {reveal link: 'RED', passage: 'RED'}
[if system[2] == 1]
  {reveal link: 'GREEN', passage: 'GREEN'}
[if system[2] == 2]

[if system[3] == 0]
  {reveal link: 'RED', passage: 'RED'}
[if system[3] == 1]
  {reveal link: 'GREEN', passage: 'GREEN'}

```
[if system[3] == 2]
  <br>
```


:: RED
REPORT
[JavaScript]

```
  let percentage = Math.randomRange(0, 11);
  let foundHealth;
  let foundFuel;
  let health = engine.state.get('health');
  let fuel = engine.state.get('fuel');

  if(percentage >= 6) {

    foundHealth = Math.randomRange(1, 6);
    foundFuel = Math.randomRange(1, 3);

    write(`The hostile environment damaged the ship, but extra fuel was found. (-${foundHealth} to health and +${foundFuel} to fuel.)`);

    health -= foundHealth;
    fuel += foundFuel;

  }

  if(percentage >= 3 && percentage < 6) {

      foundHealth = Math.randomRange(2, 8);

      write(`A hostile ship attacked. (-${foundHealth} to health)`);

      health -= foundHealth;

  }

  if(percentage < 3) {
    write("Nothing happened.");
```

```
  }

  engine.state.set('health', health);
  engine.state.set('fuel', fuel);
[continued]
{embed passage: "CheckStatus"}

:: GREEN
REPORT
[JavaScript]
  let percentage = Math.randomRange(0, 11);
  let foundFuel = 0;
  let foundHealth = 0;
  let fuel = engine.state.get('fuel');
  let health = engine.state.get('health');


  if(percentage < 2) {

    foundFuel = Math.randomRange(1,3);
    write(`Fuel was found in some wreckage. (+${foundFuel} to fuel)`);
    fuel += foundFuel;

  }

  if(percentage > 6) {

    foundHealth = Math.randomRange(1,4);
    write(`During a brief pause, the ship was able to be repaired. (+${foundHealth} to health)`);
    health += foundHealth;

  }

  if(percentage > 2 && percentage < 6)
  {
    write(`Nothing happened.`);
  }
```

```
  engine.state.set('health', health);
  engine.state.set('fuel', fuel);
[continued]
{embed passage: "CheckStatus"}

:: Statistics
Health: {health}

Fuel: {fuel}

Number of Jumps Left: {numberOfJumpsLeft}

[[Explore Space]]
```

Static Healthbars

Summary

"Static Healthbars" demonstrates how to write HTML elements that use JavaScript in Chapbook by including the **[JavaScript]** modifier in a passage. Chapbook also provides the **engine.state.get()** and **engine.state.set()** functions for getting and setting story variables.

Using these and the **write()** function, dynamic values can be created, accessed, and combined to produce static "healthbars" using the **<progress>** and **<meter>** HTML elements.

Twee Code

```
:: StoryTitle
Chapbook: Static Healthbars

:: Start
[JavaScript]
  // Create a global variable, health
  engine.state.set('health', 80);

  // Get the current value of 'health'
  let health = engine.state.get('health');

  // Write description
  write("Show a healthbar using a Progress element:<br>");

  // Write the progress element with dynamic value
  write('<progress value="' + health + '" max="100"></progress><br>');

  // Write description
  write("Show a healthbar using a Meter element:<br>");

  // Write the meter element with dynamic value
  write('<meter value="' + health + '" min="0" max="100"></meter>');
```

Story and Passage API

Summary

Often, it can be useful to access information about a Story or another passage while the Story is running. In Chapbook, the *engine.story* object provides two functions, **passageNamed()** and **passageWithId()**, for accessing other passages. Combined with the [JavaScript] modifier, these functions and values they return when given existing passage names, can be used to show the name and source of one passage in another.

Twee Code

```
:: StoryTitle
Chapbook: Story and Passage API

:: Start
The title of this story is "{story.name}".

The title of this passage is "{passage.name}".

[JavaScript]
  // Find a passage by name
  let storagePassage = engine.story.passageNamed("Storage");

  // Write the name
  write('The name of the passage is "' + storagePassage.name + '".<br>');

  // Write the source
  write('The name of the passage is "' + storagePassage.source + '".<br>');

:: Storage
This is content in the storage passage!
```

Style Markup

Summary

Chapbook uses a customized sub-set of Markdown to support its style formatting.

Twee Code

```
:: StoryTitle
Style Markup in Chapbook

:: Start
*Emphasis (aka Italics)* or _using single underscores_ <br>
**Strong Emphasis (aka Bold)** or __using double underscores__ <br>
Combined Emphasis with **asterisks and _underscores_** <br>
<del>Strikethrough text</del> <br>
Super<sup>script</sup> <br>
Sub<sub>script</sub> <br>
`Monospaced Type (aka Code Block)` <br>
~~Small Caps~~
<blockquote>Quote</blockquote>

* A Bulleted list item (using asterisk)
* Another Bulleted list item (using asterisk)
- A Bulleted list item (using minus)
- Another Bulleted list item (using minus)
+ A Bulleted list item (using plus)
+ Another Bulleted list item (using plus)

1. A Numbered list item
2. Another Numbered list item

[align left]
Text is left-aligned.
[align center]
```

Text is centered / centred.
[align right]
Text is right-aligned.
[Continue]
Text-alignment has been reset to the default.

Ignoring of *Formatting* Characters
More ignoring of __Formatting__ Characters

Above Section Break is Chapbook specific or standard HTML...
***
Below Section Break is supported Markdown extras...

Level 1 Heading
Level 2 Heading
Level 3 Heading
Level 4 Heading
Level 5 Heading
Level 6 Heading

Alternative Level 1 Heading
======
Alternative Level 2 Heading

Table mark-up	with	alignment
column 1 is	left-aligned	1
col 2 is	centered	10
col 3 is	right-aligned	100

Timed Passages

Summary

Made famous in *Queers in Love at the End of the World* (2013), "Timed Passages" uses the JavaScript function **setTimeout()** and Chapbook's internal **go()** function to reload a passage every second. It combines the use of the Vars Section with multiple modifiers.

Twee Code

```
:: StoryTitle
Chapbook: Timed Passages

:: Start
timeLeft: 11
--
[[Start->Timer]]

:: World End
The world ended.

:: Timer
timeLeft: timeLeft - 1
--
[if timeLeft > 0]
  There are {timeLeft} seconds left.
[else]
  {embed passage: 'World End'}
[JavaScript]
  window.setTimeout(() => go('Timer'), 1000);
```

Turn Counter

Summary

In Chapbook, the global variable *trail* stores all of the passages visited as an increasing array. For each passage visited, a new entry is added.

Sometimes known as "wrap around," the modulus operator (%) is used to get the remainder of the number of "turns" (number of passages) divided by 24. This creates a clock where its value shows one of a series of strings representing "morning," "mid-morning," "afternoon," or "night."

By visiting other passages, the turn count is increased and the hour reaches 23 before being reset back to 0 before increasing again.

Twee Code

```
:: StoryTitle
Chapbook: Turn Counter

:: Start
hour: trail.length % 24
--
{embed passage: "Turn Counter"}
Rooms:

[[Back Room]]

[[Left Room]]

[[Right Room]]


:: Back Room
{embed passage: "Turn Counter"}
Rooms:
```

[[Left Room]]

[[Right Room]]

[[Front Room|Start]]

:: Left Room
{embed passage: "Turn Counter"}
Rooms:

[[Right Room]]

[[Back Room]]

[[Front Room|Start]]

:: Right Room
{embed passage: "Turn Counter"}
Rooms:

[[Left Room]]

[[Back Room]]

[[Front Room|Start]]

:: Turn Counter
hour: trail.length % 24
--
[if hour <= 8]
　It is morning.

[if hour > 8 && hour <= 12]
　It is mid-morning.

[if hour > 12 && hour <= 16]
　It is afternoon.

```
[if hour > 16]
  It is night.
```

Typewriter Effect

Summary

"Typewriter Effect" demonstrates how to create a delayed character-by-character effect. In Chapbook, new modifiers can be added through the *engine.extend()* function. This examples creates a new modifier called **[typewriter]** that accepts a time in milliseconds.

The **[typewriter]** modifier creates a series of **<span>** elements for each character found within the output of the modifier and sets an **animation-delay** equal to the time given to the modifier multiplied by the position of the character within the total length of the text output. When used, each character will appear within the passage as if "typed" based on the time given to the modifier.

Twee Code

```
:: StoryTitle
Chapbook: Typewriter

:: Start
[JavaScript]
engine.extend('1.0.0', () => {
    config.template.modifiers = [{
        match: /^typewriter\s/i,
        process(output, {invocation}) {
        // Get the time
        let time = invocation.replace(/^typewriter\s/i, '');

        // Save original text
        let text = output.text;

        // Get length of original text
        let length = text.length;

        // Set initial index
```

```
        let index = 0;

        // Wipe out output to start
        output.text = "";

        // Loop through the text
        //   -- Add a new <span> for each character
        //   -- Set the class "fade-in"
        //   -- Set the delay as equal to time multiplied position
        for(let i = 0; i < length; i++) {
          output.text += `<span class='fade-in' style='animation-delay: ${time * i} ms'>${text[i]}</span>`;
        }


        }
    }, ...config.template.modifiers];
});
[continued]
[[Start TypeWriter]]

:: Start TypeWriter
[typewriter 1000]
Hello, world!
[continued]
```

Variable Story Styling

Summary

Using the **[CSS]** modifier in Chapbook, it is possible to combine expressions with variables and change the text and background colors dynamically. This examples creates a variable *color* and changes its value in the Vars Section of two passages.

Twee Code

```
:: StoryTitle
Chapbook: Variable Story Styling

:: Start
color: "green"
--

[CSS]
#page article {
    color: {color};
}

[continued]
This text will be in green.

[[Switch to red text]]

:: Switch to red text
color: "red"
--
[CSS]
#page article {
    color: {color};
}
```

[continued]
This text will be in red.

[[Switch to green text->Start]]

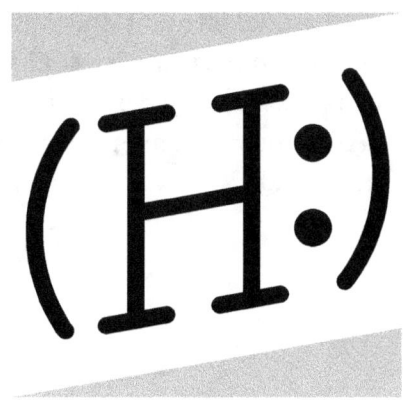

Harlowe

Arrays

Summary

Arrays are a collection of values. Each entry in an array is assigned an *index*, which is a number that corresponds to its position in the array. Unlike in JavaScript, arrays are one-based in Harlowe, meaning the first element in the array is given the index "1". Arrays can be created using the **(a:)** or **(array:)** macro and assigning a variable to it: **(set: $myArray to (a:))**.

Specific elements in an array can be accessed by following its variable name with a possessive **'s** and an ordinal number referencing the index to check, such as **$myArray's 2nd**. The final entry, **$myArray's last**, points to the final element. Its contents can be tested using the **contains** operator (e.g. **(if: $myArray contains 'something')[...]**), new items can be added using the **+** operator (e.g. **(set: $myArray to + (a: 'something'))**), and items can be removed using the **-** operator. All elements in an array can be passed to macros as separate arguments with the spread operator (**...**).

Twee Code

```
:: StoryTitle
Arrays in Harlowe

:: init [startup]
<!-- it is always a good idea to initialize your variables, but with arrays it is
particularly important -->
(set: $inventory to (a:))
(set: $chest to (a: 'a shield', 'a suit of armor'))
(set: $chestOpen to false)

:: inventory [header]
You are currently carrying:
<!-- if the inventory contains nothing, show "nothing" -->\
(if: $inventory's length is 0)[\
    nothing.
](else:)[\
```

Conditional Statements

Summary

The **(if:)** and **(else:)** macros conditionally produce commands that can be attached to hooks in Harlowe. If the statement is true, the **(if:)** section will be run. Otherwise, the **(else:)** section will be.

The **(unless:)** macro can also be used in place of **(if:)** for the opposite effect. Furthermore, variables can be attached to hooks to control whether they are displayed based on if they are "true" (will be displayed) or "false" (will not be displayed).

Twee Code

```
:: StoryTitle
Conditional Statements in Harlowe

:: Start
(set: $animal to "horse")

(if: $animal is "dog")[It's a dog!]
(else:)[It's a horse!]

(unless: $animal is "dog")[It's a horse!]
(else:)[It's a dog!]

(set: $isDog to $animal is "horse")
$isDog[It's a dog!]
```

See Also

Harlowe: Setting and Showing Variables (pg. 176)

CSS Selectors

> **Warning**
> The following example is designed for use in Harlowe 2.x and later.

Summary

This example shows how to use CSS selectors to style different areas of the page. In Harlowe, custom HTML elements are used for layout: the **<tw-story>** element contains the page as well as an element containing the currently shown passage, **<tw-passage>**, and an element containing the sidebar, **<tw-sidebar>**.

```
<tw-story>
  <tw-passage>
    <tw-sidebar>...</tw-sidebar>
    ...
  </tw-passage>
</tw-story>
```

Twee Code

```
:: StoryTitle
CSS Selectors in Harlowe

:: UserStylesheet [stylesheet]
tw-story {
    border: 5px solid lightgreen;
}

tw-sidebar {
    border: 2px solid blue;
}

tw-passage {
    border: 1px solid red;
```

```
        <!-- we iterate over the array and print each item -->\
        (for: each _item, ...$inventory)[\
            _item (unless: $inventory's last is _item)[, ]\
        ].
]
-----


:: Start
<!-- we use the + operator and wrap the target elements in an (a:) macro to add to the
array -->\
You find yourself inside a small room. In the corner, you see a sword, and decide to pick
it up.

(set: $inventory to it + (a: 'a sword'))\
[[Continue|hallway]]

:: hallway
You see a chest here in the hallway.  \
(unless: $chestOpen)[\
    Do you want to open it?

    {
    (link: 'Open the chest.')[
        <!-- adding to arrays together can also be done with the + operator -->
        (set: $inventory to it + $chest)
        (set: $chestOpen to true)
        (goto: 'chest')
    ]
    }
](else:)[\
    It's open, and there's nothing inside.
]\

[[Move on.|dart trap]]

:: chest
You open the chest and find (for: each _item, ...$chest)[\
    _item (unless: $chest's last is _item)[ and ]\
].
```

```
}

:: Start
The page has a green border; it contains this passage (red border) and the sidebar
(blue border).
[[Second]]

:: Second
This passage also has a red border.
```

See Also

Styling custom elements like <tw-sidebar>
Harlowe: Left Sidebar (pg. 156)

Styling passages by tag using Harlowe's custom 'tags' attribute
Harlowe: CSS and Passage Tags (pg. 134)

CSS and Passage Tags

> **Warning**
> The following example is designed for use in Harlowe 2.x and later.

Summary

This example shows how to use CSS selectors to selectively style different passages based on how they are tagged. In Harlowe, the "tags" attribute can be used to create different sets of styles and apply them when shown.

Twee Code

```
:: StoryTitle
CSS and Passage Tags in Harlowe

:: UserStylesheet[stylesheet]
[tags="grey"] {
    background: grey;
}

[tags="yellow"] {
    background: yellow;
    color: black;
}

:: Start[grey]
This passage has a grey background and (default) white text.
[[Second]]

:: Second[yellow]
This passage has a yellow background and black text.
```

Cycling Choices

Summary

Starting in Harlowe 3.0.1, the **(cycling-link)** macro was introduced. Clicking on the link it provides allows for cycling though its possibilities. Combined with the **bind** keyword, its selection can be saved to a variable.

Twee Code

```
:: StoryTitle
Harlowe 3: Cycling Links

:: Start
This cycling-link example remembers the choice made:
(cycling-link: bind $hair, "Black", "Brown", "Blonde", "Red", "White")

This cycling-link example does not:
(cycling-link: "Cat", "Dog", "Fish", "Mouse")

This cycling-link example will disappear (show empty string) on its last choice:
(cycling-link: "Two eggs", "One egg", "")

[[Show result]]

:: Show result
The choice of hair was $hair.
```

See Also

Harlowe: Modularity (pg. 163), Setting and Showing Variables (pg. 176)

Date and Time

Summary

"Date and Time" demonstrates how to use the **(current-date:)**, **(current-time:)**, and other time-related macros in Harlowe.

Twee Code

```
:: StoryTitle
Date and Time in Harlowe

:: Start
The current date is (current-date:).
The current time is (current-time: ).
The current day (of the month) is (monthday: ).
The current day is (weekday: ).
```

Delayed Text

Summary

"Delayed Text" uses the **(live:)** and **(stop:)** macros to create a loop that runs only once with a delay of five seconds.

Twee Code

```
:: StoryTitle
Delayed Text in Harlowe

:: Start
{
 (live: 5s)[
    (stop:)
    It has been 5 seconds. Show the text!
 ]
}
```

See Also

Harlowe: Typewriter Effect (pg. 192)

Dice Rolling

Summary

"Dice Rolling" demonstrates how to create the same effects of rolling various physical dice through using the **(random:)** macro and adding or subtracting numbers.

Twee Code

```
:: StoryTitle
Harlowe: Dice Rolling

:: Start
Rolling a 1d4: (random: 1,4)
Rolling a 1d6: (random: 1,6)
Rolling a 1d8: (random: 1,8)
Rolling a 1d10: (random: 1, 10)
Rolling a 1d12: (random: 1, 12)
Rolling a 1d20: (random: 1, 20)
Rolling a 1d100: (random: 1, 100)
Rolling a 1d4 + 4: (text: (random: 1, 4) + 4)
Rolling a 1d6 - 2: (text: (random: 1, 6) - 2)
Rolling a 2d6 + 10: (text: (random: 1, 6) + (random: 1, 6) + 10)
```

Dropdown

Summary

The macro **(dropdown:)** was introduced with Harlowe 3.0. It creates a drop-down menu based on the options supplied to it. In order to save the outcome of using the drop-down menu, the keyword **bind** is used to save the choice.

Twee Code

```
:: StoryTitle
Harlowe 3: Dropdown

:: Start
Choose direction:
(dropdown: bind $direction, "Up", "Down", "Left", "Right")

[[Show result]]

:: Show result
The direction picked was $direction.
```

Fairmath System

Summary

"Fairmath System" demonstrates how to re-create the Fairmath system found in ChoiceScript. Based on a percentage operation, increasing and decreasing changes the value by a percentage as the difference between the original and adjusted value.

This example uses the **(display:)** macro in Harlowe to separate operations for increasing and decreasing. Through setting values to adjust, either passage can be included and the variable *$resultValue* can be used to track and store changes.

Twee Code

```
:: StoryTitle
Fairmath System in Harlowe

:: Start
<!-- Fairmath formulas based on http://choicescriptdev.wikia.com/wiki/Arithmetic_operators#Fairmath -->

<!-- Set an initial value for the story -->
(set: $valueToAdjust to 100)
The initial value is $valueToAdjust.

<!-- Set originalValue to the value to adjust -->
(set: $originalValue to $valueToAdjust)
<!-- Set the changeValue (percentage) to adjust -->
(set: $changeValue to 50)
<!-- Display (call) the Fairmath Decrease passage -->
(display: "Decrease")
<!-- The new value will be resultValue -->
The adjusted value is $resultValue.

<!-- Update valueToAdjust -->
```

```
(set: $valueToAdjust to $resultValue)
<!-- Set originalValue to the value to adjust -->
(set: $originalValue to $valueToAdjust)
<!-- Set the changeValue (percentage) to adjust -->
(set: $changeValue to 100)
<!-- Display (call) the Fairmath Increase passage -->
(display: "Increase")
The adjusted value is $resultValue.

:: Increase
(set: $resultValue to (round: $originalValue+((100-$originalValue)*($changeValue/100))) )

:: Decrease
(set: $resultValue to (round: $originalValue-($originalValue*($changeValue/100)) ) )
```

Geolocation

Summary

Many browsers allow access to the user's current location through the Geolocation property and associated functions. This functionality is subject to the user agreeing to allow access. Until the functionality is unlocked, or if the user declines, default values will be returned.

Functionality availability and their results should always be tested against other location services or information. Most browsers will return results through the fastest and sometimes least-accurate methods possible.

Harlowe does not have an easy way to bridge the gap between its macros and JavaScript. In this example, the **<script>** element is used to test for, run, and show an **alert()** with data from the JavaScript functions.

Twee Code

```
:: StoryTitle
Geolocation in Harlowe

:: UserScript[script]
(function () {

  window.geolocation = {

    available: function() {
      return ("geolocation" in navigator
        && typeof navigator.geolocation.getCurrentPosition === "function");
    },
    getLocation: function() {

      // Create initial values
      var location = { latitude : 0, longitude : 0 };
```

```
    // Create success callback to store values
    var  positionSuccess = function (position) {

      location.latitude = position.coords.latitude;
      location.longitude = position.coords.longitude;

    };

    // Create error callback
    var positionError = function (error) {
      /* Code that handles errors */
    };

    // Create initial options
    var positionOptions = {
      timeout: 31000,
      enableHighAccuracy: true,
      maximumAge : 120000
    };


    // Ask for location based on callbacks and options
    navigator.geolocation.getCurrentPosition(
      positionSuccess,
      positionError,
      positionOptions
    );

    // Return location found
    // If not location, will return initial (0,0) values
    return location;

},
approximateLocation: function (a, b, allowedDiff) {
    // allowedDiff must always be > 0
  if (a === b) { // handles various "exact" edge cases
    return true;
  }
```

```
        allowedDiff = allowedDiff || 0.0005;

        return Math.abs(a - b) < allowedDiff;
    }

  };

}());

:: Start
[[Ask for permission]]

:: Ask for permission
<script>
if(window.geolocation.available() ) {
  var geolocation = window.geolocation.getLocation();
  alert("Latitude: " + geolocation.latitude + " Longitude:" + geolocation.longitude);
}
</script>
```

Google Fonts

Summary

"Google Fonts" uses a Google Font loaded via the CSS **@import** at-rule. The loaded font is then applied to selected text using the **(font:)** macro.

Other Google Fonts could be imported and applied using the same method, creating new class or ID style rules to be applied for and across different HTML elements in the same way.

Twee Code

```
:: StoryTitle
Harlowe: Google Fonts

:: StoryStylesheet[stylesheet]
@import url('https://fonts.googleapis.com/css?family=Roboto');

:: Start
(font:"Roboto")[This text is styled by a Google Font]
```

Headers and Footers

Summary

"Headers and Footers" demonstrates the use of the "header" and "footer" passage tags. When used in passages, they are either prepended (header) or appended (footer) to every passage. Multiple passages can have the tags and are loaded alphabetically when detected.

Twee Code

```
:: StoryTitle
Harlowe: Headers and Footers

:: Start
This is content between the header and the footer.


:: Header[header]
This is the header!


:: Footer[footer]
This is the footer!
```

Hidden Link

Summary

"Hidden Link" demonstrates how to create a 'hidden' link that is only revealed when the cursor passes over it.

Using CSS and JavaScript, a rule is created for transparent color and applied or removed through using jQuery's **on()** function with 'mouseenter' and 'mouseleave' events.

The use of a "footer" special passage is also used to run the required JavaScript after each passage is displayed.

Harlowe supports a number of different techniques for creating links and the resulting HTML elements generated are different for each of these techniques. The generated HTML falls into two main groups: those that include a **<<tw-link>>** element, and those that include a ".enchantment-link" classed element. This example supports both groups.

Twee Code

```
:: StoryTitle
Harlowe: Hidden Link


:: UserStylesheet [stylesheet]
.hidden tw-link, .hidden .enchantment-link {
  color: transparent;
}

tw-include[title="Hidden Link Setup"] {
  display: none;
}
```

```
:: Hidden Link Setup [footer]
<script>
  /*
     Hidden links that are always hidden:
        <span class="hidden">[[A hidden link]]</span>
  */
  $('.hidden')
    .addClass('hidden');

  /*
     Hidden links that hide unless you're hovering over them:
        <span class="hides">[[A hidden link]]</span>
  */
  $('.hides')
    .addClass('hidden')
    .on('mouseenter', function () {
      $(this).removeClass('hidden');
    })
    .on('mouseleave', function () {
      $(this).addClass('hidden');
    });

  /*
     Hidden links that reveal themselves when you hover over them:
        <span class="reveals">[[A hidden link]]</span>
  */
  $('.reveals')
    .addClass('hidden')
    .one('mouseenter', function () {
      $(this).removeClass('hidden');
    });
</script>
```

```
:: Start
''Examples of tw-link element based links''

A hidden link that's always hidden: <span class="hidden">[[A hidden link]]</span>

A hidden link that hides unless you're hovering over it: <span class="hides">[[A hidden link]]</span>

A hidden link that reveals itself when you hover over it: <span class="reveals">[[A hidden link]]</span>


''Examples of .enchantment-link CSS class based links''

A hidden link that's always hidden: <span class="hidden">[A hidden link]<link|</span>

A hidden link that hides unless you're hovering over it: <span class="hides">[A hidden link]<link|</span>

A hidden link that reveals itself when you hover over it: <span class="reveals">[A hidden link]<link|</span>

(click: ?link)[(go-to: "A hidden link")]


:: A hidden link
You found it!
```

Images

Summary

When using Harlowe, images can be displayed through the image HTML element and **url()** CSS data type when encoded as Base64.

When using an image element, its source is either absolutely or relatively located. An absolute reference starts with HTTP or another protocol; a relative reference describes the location of the image in relation to the webpage.

Because images are external resources, they need to be included with the webpage as Base64-encoded or in another location. While Base64-encoded images can be embedded in a webpage, it also increases its overall size. External images require additional hosting and are included through their reference in CSS (URL) data type or image (SRC) attribute.

Twee Code

```
:: StoryTitle
Images in Harlowe

:: UserStylesheet[stylesheet]
.base64image {
  width: 256px;
  height: 256px;
  /* Base64 image truncated for example */
  /* See Twee file for full version. */
  background-image: url('data:image/png;base64...');
}

:: Start
This is an image element:

<img src="https://twinery.org/homepage/img/logo.svg" width="256" height="256">
```

This is a base-64-encoded CSS image background:

```
<div class="base64image"></div>
```

Importing External JavaScript

> **Information**
> The successful loading of an external JavaScript file or library commonly produces no visual output. The code within the example passage is not required for the successful loading of an external file or library.

Summary

"Importing External JavaScript" demonstrates how to import an externally stored JavaScript library, jQuery UI.

This example uses the built-in jQuery **$.getScript()** function to load the library and demonstrates a short example of how to use it.

Twee Code

```
:: StoryTitle
Harlowe: Importing External JavaScript


:: UserScript [script]
/* import jQuery UI library. */
$(function () {
  $.getScript("https://ajax.googleapis.com/ajax/libs/jqueryui/1.12.1/jquery-ui.min.js",
    function (data, textStatus, jqxhr) {
      console.log('jquery ui file loaded');
    }
  );
});
```

```
:: Start
<p>Click on the grey box below to see it bounce.</p>
<div id="box" style="width: 100px; height: 100px; background: #ccc;"></div>

<script>
$("#box").click(function () {
  $("#box").toggle("bounce", {times: 3}, "slow");
});
</script>
```

Keyboard Events

Summary

"Keyboard Events" demonstrates how to capture keyboard events and then how to associate individual keys with activities within a story.

The example uses jQuery's **on()** function to monitor for all *keyup* events. Once a "keyup" event has occurred, two values are available:

- The *keyCode* property: the numerical value representing the key presented in its decimal ASCII code supported by effectively all browsers.
- The *key* property: the string value of the key presented supported by most modern web-browsers.

Twee Code

```
:: StoryTitle
Harlowe: Keyboard


:: UserScript[script]
(function () {
  $(document).on('keyup', function (ev) {
    /* the ev variable contains a keyup event object.
     *
     * ev.keyCode - contains the ASCII code of the key that was released, this property is supported in effectively all browsers.
     * ev.key     - contains the key value of the key that was released, this property is supported by most modern browsers.
     *
     */


    /* the following shows an alert when the 'a' key is released. */
```

```
    if (ev.key === 'a') {
      alert("the 'a' key was released.");
    }
  });
}());
```

:: Start
Press and release the "a" key to show an Alert dialog.

Left Sidebar

Summary

Harlowe v2.1.0 or later includes a built-in named hook named *?Sidebar*. When combined with the **(append:)** macro, dynamic content can be added to the left, blank area containing the default Undo and Redo links. A "footer" tagged passage is used to update the dynamic content after each passage transition, and CSS is used to resize and position the existing `<tw-sidebar>` element.

Twee Code

```
:: StoryTitle
Left Sidebar in Harlowe (v2.1.0 or later)

:: UserStylesheet [stylesheet]
/*
  Reposition the Sidebar 'footer' tagged passage.
*/
tw-sidebar {
  position: fixed;
  top: 0;
  left: 0;
  width: 20%; /* padding-right of the tw-story element. */
  max-height: 100%;
  margin-top: 5%; /* padding-top of the tw-story element. */
  padding: 0 0.5em 0.5em 0.5em;
  text-align: right;
  background-color: transparent;
}
tw-icon {
  text-align: right;
  padding-right: 0.75em;
}
```

```
:: Start
(set: $name to "Jane Doe", $location to "Work")\
[[Another passage]]

:: Sidebar [footer]
(append: ?SideBar)[\
Name: $name
Location: $location
]

:: Another passage
(set: $name to "John Smith", $location to "Shop")\
[[Start]]
```

See Also

Harlowe: CSS and Passage Tags (pg. 133)

Lock and Key: Variable

> **Information**
> This example is affected by history changes in the story. Undoing or re-doing back to a passage containing this recipe has the potential to change its saved values.

Summary

"Lock and Key: Variable" demonstrates how to create the effect of picking up a key and unlocking a door. In this example, the key is a variable (*$key*) and is initially set to the value "false" in the Start passage.

When the link "Pick up the key" is clicked, *$key* is changed to the value "true" and the door link changes from its initial response of "Locked Door" to a link to the passage Exit.

Twee Code

```
:: StoryTitle
Lock and Key: Variable in Harlowe

:: Start
(set: $key to false)

Rooms:
[[Front Room]]
[[Back Room]]

:: Front Room
(if: $key is true)[
  [[Exit]]
]
(else:)[
  *Locked Door*
]
```

```
Rooms:
[[Back Room]]

:: Back Room
(if: $key is false)[
  Items:
  (link: "Pick up key")[(set: $key to true)You have a key.]
]
(else:)[
  There is nothing here.
]

Rooms:
[[Front Room]]

:: Exit
You found the key and went through the door!
```

See Also

Harlowe: Setting and Showing Variables (pg. 176)

Looping

Summary

In programming terminology, a "loop" is a common technique for iterating (moving through one by one) some type of data. In Harlowe, the macros **(loop:)** and **(for:)** provide this functionality. When combined with the keywords **each**, to move through all entries, or **where**, to specify some condition, they allow for "looping" through data structures like arrays or datamaps.

In this example, the variable *arrayInventory* is set to the value of an array containing the strings "Bread", "Pan", and "Book". The **(for:)** macro is used with the keyword **each** to set the values contained in the array to the temporary variable *_temp* for each value of the spread out array. The text contained in the hook associated to the **(for:)** macro is shown during each loop with the value of *_temp* changed for each value in the array.

Twee Code

```
:: StoryTitle
Looping in Harlowe

:: Start
<!-- Create an array of the strings "Bread", "Pan", "Book" -->
(set: $arrayInventory to (a: "Bread", "Pan", "Book") )

<!-- For each entry in the expanded array in turn, -->
<!-- set the entry to the temporary variable _temp -->
(for: each _temp, ...$arrayInventory)[
You have _temp.]
```

Modal (Pop-up Window)

Summary

This example creates a re-usable modal window. It can be opened using the combination of **(link-repeat:)** and **(replace:)** to create the window in an existing hook, and be 'closed' using the same macros to remove the window. CSS rules are applied with **(css:)** to style the modal, and to change an enclosing hook into a "dimmer" which obscures the rest of the page.

Twee Code

```
:: StoryTitle
Harlowe: Modal

:: Header[header]
|modalhooks>[]

:: Modal code
(replace: ?modalhooks)[{
  (css:"
  position: fixed;
  display:block;
  z-index: 1;
  left: 0;
  top: 0;
  width: 100%; /* Full width */
  height: 100%; /* Full height */
  overflow: auto; /* Enable scroll if needed */
  background-color: rgba(0,0,0,0.4);
  ")[
  (css:"
    display:block;
    margin: 15% auto;
    padding: 20px;
    width: 80%;
```

```
      border: 1px solid white;
   ")|modal>[
      (css:"float:right")+(link-repeat:"×")[(replace: ?modalhooks)[]]
   ]
  ]
}]

:: Start
(link-repeat:"Open Modal!")[(display:"Modal code")(append:?modal)[Some text in the
modal...]]
```

Modularity

Summary

In programming terminology, modularity refers to dividing software into different sections related to their purpose or to better organize the whole. In Harlowe, this technique can be used through the **(display:)** macro to print the contents of one passage in another. Parts of a story can often be re-used in this way.

Twee Code

```
:: StoryTitle
Modularity in Harlowe

:: Start
(set: $lineOne to "Give us a verse")
(set: $lineTwo to "Drop some knowledge")

(display: "showLineOne")
(display: "showLineTwo")

:: showLineOne
$lineOne

:: showLineTwo
$lineTwo
```

Moving through a dungeon

Summary

"Moving through a 'dungeon'" uses the **(array:)** macro to create a multidimensional array. Movement positions are then tracked through X and Y variables for a grid system. Each movement subtracts or adds to its corresponding X or Y position and is compared to those same positions within the array. Different directions are shown if movement is possible in that direction.

A map of the array is created by iterating through temporary variables and placing different symbols matching walls, movement spaces, and the player herself.

Twee Code

```
:: StoryTitle
Harlowe: Moving through Dungeons


:: User Style [stylesheet]
tw-include[type="startup"], tw-hook[name="workarea"] {
  display: none;
}
tw-hook[name="map"] {
  font-family: monospace;
  line-height: 1.75;
  font-size: 16pt;
}


:: Start
|map>[(display: "Map")]
```

```
:: Map
(set: $map to "")\
|workarea>[
  (for: each _y, ...(range: 1, $dungeon's length))[
    (for: each _x, ...(range: 1, $dungeon's (_y)'s length))[
      (if: _x is $positionX and _y is $positionY)[
        (set: $map to it + "P ")
      ]
      (else-if: $dungeon's (_y)'s (_x) is 0)[
        (set: $map to it + "&num; ")
      ]
      (else-if: $dungeon's (_y)'s (_x) is 1)[
        (set: $map to it + ". ")
      ]
      (else-if: $dungeon's (_y)'s (_x) is 2)[
        (set: $map to it + "E ")
      ]
    ]
    (set: $map to it + " <br>")
  ]
]\
$map

{
  (set: $separator to "")\
  (set: _north to $dungeon's ($positionY - 1)'s ($positionX))
  (set: _east to $dungeon's ($positionY)'s ($positionX + 1))
  (set: _south to $dungeon's ($positionY + 1)'s ($positionX))
  (set: _west to $dungeon's ($positionY)'s ($positionX - 1))

  (if: _north is 1)[
    $separator
    (link: "North")[
      (set: $positionY to it - 1)
      (replace: ?map)[(display: "Map")]
    ]
    (set: $separator to " | ")
  ]
```

```
(else-if: _north is 2)[
  $separator[[Exit]]
  (set: $separator to " | ")
]

(if: _east is 1)[
  $separator
  (link: "East")[
    (set: $positionX to it + 1)
    (replace: ?map)[(display: "Map")]
  ]
  (set: $separator to " | ")
]
(else-if: _east is 2)[
  $separator[[Exit]]
  (set: $separator to " | ")
]

(if: _south is 1)[
  $separator
  (link: "South")[
    (set: $positionY to it + 1)
    (replace: ?map)[(display: "Map")]
  ]
  (set: $separator to " | ")
]
(else-if: _south is 2)[
  $separator[[Exit]]
  (set: $separator to " | ")
]

(if: _west is 1)[
  $separator
  (link: "West")[
    (set: $positionX to it - 1)
    (replace: ?map)[(display: "Map")]
  ]
]
```

```
      (else-if: _west is 2)[
        $separator[[Exit]]
      ]
  }
}


:: Startup [startup]
{
  (set: $dungeon to (array:
      (a: 0,0,0,0,0,0,0,0,0,0,0),
      (a: 0,1,1,1,0,1,1,1,1,1,0),
      (a: 0,0,0,1,0,0,0,0,0,1,0),
      (a: 0,1,0,1,1,1,1,1,0,1,0),
      (a: 0,1,0,0,0,0,0,1,0,1,0),
      (a: 0,1,1,1,1,1,1,1,0,1,0),
      (a: 0,0,0,0,0,0,0,1,0,1,0),
      (a: 0,1,0,1,1,1,1,1,1,1,0),
      (a: 0,1,0,1,0,0,0,1,0,0,0),
      (a: 0,1,1,1,0,1,1,1,1,2,0),
      (a: 0,0,0,0,0,0,0,0,0,0,0)
    )
  )
    (set: $positionX to 2)
    (set: $positionY to 2)
}


:: Exit
You have exited the map.
```

See Also

> Harlowe: Conditional Statements (pg. 130), Modularity (pg. 163), Setting and Showing Variables (pg. 176)

Passages in Passages

Summary

The Harlowe story format allows for content from one passage to be displayed in another passage through the use of the **(display:)** macro. Given the name of an existing passage, its contents will added wherever the macro is called.

Twee Code

```
:: StoryTitle
Harlowe: Passages in Passages

:: Start
This is the Start passage!
(display: "Another")

:: Another
And this is another passage!
```

Passage Transitions

Summary

When using the **(transition-arrive:)** or **(transition-depart:)** macros with links, the specified transition effect will be shown to the player upon activating the link (depart) or as it the contents of the link are shown (arrive).

Possible transition effects include:

- "instant" (causes the passage to instantly vanish)
- "dissolve" (causes the passage to gently fade in or out)
- "flicker" (causes the passage to roughly flicker in - don't use with a long **(transition-time:)**)
- "shudder" (causes the passage to appear or disappear while shaking left and right)
- "rumble" (causes the passage to instantly appear or disappear while shaking up and down)
- "slide-right" (causes the passage to slide in or out from the right)
- "slide-left" (causes the passage to slide in or out from the left)
- "pulse" (causes the passage to appear or disappear while pulsating rapidly)

Twee Code

```
:: StoryTitle
Harlowe 3: Passage Transitions

:: Start
(transition-depart: "dissolve")[[Dissolve Passage]]

:: Dissolve Passage
(transition-arrive: "slide-right")[[Slide-right Passage]]

:: Slide-right Passage
The slid passage.
```

Passage Visits

Summary

In Harlowe 3.1, the keyword **visits** is introduced. This value contains the number of times the current passage has been visited.

In this example, the macro **(str:)** is used with the keyword **visits** to show the value.

Twee Code

```
:: StoryTitle
Harlowe: Passage Visits

:: Start
How many times has the passage "Another Passage" been visited? (str: visits)

[[Another Passage]]

:: Another Passage
[[Start]]
```

Player Statistics

Summary

Some of the most popular mechanics from table-top role-playing games are those where the player must determine their in-game statistics and then use them to make decisions.

In this example, the **(link-repeat:)** macro is used multiple times with **(replace:)** and **(set:)** macros, while checking if the values are higher than a target number. In a second passage, these values are added to a random number between 1 to 6, mimicking the common mechanic of rolling 1d6 plus the value of a statistic to beat a target number.

Twee Code

```
:: StoryTitle
Player Statistics in Harlowe

:: Start
Empathy: {
  (link-repeat: "|+|")[
    (if: $totalPoints > 0)[
    (set: $empathy to it + 1)
    (set: $totalPoints to it - 1)
    (replace: ?empathyStat)[|empathyStat>[$empathy]]
    (replace: ?pointsStat)[|pointsStat>[$totalPoints]]
    ]
  ]

  (link-repeat: "|-|")[
    (if: $empathy > 0)[
    (set: $empathy to it - 1)
    (set: $totalPoints to it + 1)
    (replace: ?empathyStat)[|empathyStat>[$empathy]]
    (replace: ?pointsStat)[|pointsStat>[$totalPoints]]
    ]
  ]
}
```

```
Intelligence: {
  (link-repeat: "|+|")[
    (if: $totalPoints > 0)[
    (set: $intelligence to it + 1)
    (set: $totalPoints to it - 1)
    (replace: ?intelligenceStat)[|intelligenceStat>[$intelligence]]
    (replace: ?pointsStat)[|pointsStat>[$totalPoints]]
    ]
  ]

  (link-repeat: "|-|")[
    (if: $intelligence > 0)[
    (set: $intelligence to it - 1)
    (set: $totalPoints to it + 1)
    (replace: ?intelligenceStat)[|intelligenceStat>[$intelligence]]
    (replace: ?pointsStat)[|pointsStat>[$totalPoints]]
    ]
  ]
}
{
  (link-repeat: "|Reset Points|")[
    (set: $empathy to 10)
    (set: $intelligence to 10)
    (set: $totalPoints to 5)
    (replace: ?empathyStat)[|empathyStat>[$empathy]]
    (replace: ?intelligenceStat)[|intelligenceStat>[$intelligence]]
    (replace: ?pointsStat)[|pointsStat>[$totalPoints]]
  ]
}

Empathy: |empathyStat>[10]
Intelligence: |intelligenceStat>[10]
Remaining Points: |pointsStat>[5]

[[Test Stats]]

:: Test Stats
(link: "Make an intelligence check?")[
  (set: _result to (random: 1, 6) + $intelligence)
```

```
  (if: _result >= 15)[
  Intelligence Success! (_result >= 15)
  ](else:)[
  Intelligence Failure! (_result < 15)
  ]
]
(link: "Make an empathy check?")[
  (set: _result to (random: 1, 6) + $empathy)
  (if: _result >= 15)[
  Empathy Success! (_result >= 15)
  ](else:)[
  Empathy Failure! (_result < 15)
  ]
]

:: Startup[startup]
(set: $empathy to 10)
(set: $intelligence to 10)
(set: $totalPoints to 5)
```

See Also

Harlowe: Conditional Statements (pg. 129), Setting and Showing Variables (pg. 175)

Programmatic Undo

Summary

While Harlowe supports allowing the user to undo and redo moves, the "undo" operation can also be accessed through the **(undo:)** macro. Through its use, changes from the most recent action can be "undone."

Twee Code

```
:: StoryTitle
Programmatic Undo in Harlowe

:: Start
[[Enter the darkness]]

:: Enter the darkness
(link: "You are not ready. Go back!")[(undo:)]
```

Saving Games

Summary

Harlowe provides macros like **(save-game:)** and **(load-game:)** to store and retrieve game "saves" of the variables and current passage. **(saved-games:)** can also be used to check if a certain game save exists.

Game saves are stored as cookies in the user's browser. If cookies cannot be stored for some reason, games cannot be saved. It is recommended to always check if the game save was stored before trying to retrieve it later.

Twee Code

```
:: StoryTitle
Saving Games in Harlowe

:: Start
(link:"Save game?")[
  (if:(save-game:"Slot A"))[
  (if: (saved-games:) contains "Slot A")[
    Slot A is in the saved-games datamap!
  ]
  (link: "Load Slot A?" )[
     (load-game: "Slot A")
  ]
  ](else: )[
    Sorry, I couldn't save your game.
  ]
]
```

Setting and Showing Variables

Summary

Variables, symbols starting with **$** (for story-wide) or **_** (for temporary), can be "set" using the **(set:)** macro in Harlowe. The value of a variable can be shown by writing the name of that variable in the body of a passage (as in the example below).

$ is used for storing data throughout the story, and **_** should be used for data only needed in the current passage. Using **_** is useful for not wanting to accidentally overwrite variables elsewhere in the story. They can also help with debugging by not cluttering up the variables list of future passages.

In Harlowe, the keyword **it** can also be used as a shortcut for changing and saving a value in reference to itself. The **it** refers to the first variable named in the macro.

Twee Code

```
:: StoryTitle
Setting and Showing Variables in Harlowe

:: Start
(set: $numberVariable to 5)
(set: $textVariable to "five")
(set: _textVariable to "The values")

_textVariable are $numberVariable and $textVariable.

(set: $numberVariable to it + 1)

_textVariable are $numberVariable and $textVariable.
```

Space Exploration

Summary

Games in the roguelike genre often have random events that influence player choices. Depending on these random events, a player's decisions can have lasting impact or even lead to the end of a session of play.

Heavily inspired by *FTL: Faster Than Light* (2012), this example uses the **(random:)** macro to generate a system of planets consisting of either RED, more risk and more reward, or GREEN, less risk and less reward. Upon entering a system of planets, the player can choose to visit these planets and receive different events based on the outcome of another **(random:)** macro to select between several possible incidents. While traveling, the player must also balance the health of the ship, the number of jumps left, and the remaining fuel, which are all displayed using the **(display:)** macro. Finally, to capture the permanence of death many roguelike games, the **(go-to:)** macro is used to prevent the use of the undo operation to navigate away from the death screen.

Twee Code

```
:: StoryTitle
Space Exploration in Harlowe

:: Start
[[Explore Space!|Explore Space 1]]

:: Startup[startup]
(set: $health to 20)
(set: $fuel to 3)
(set: $system to (a:) )
(set: $numberOfJumpsLeft to 10)

:: Generate System
{
  <!-- Save a range from 0 to a max of 3 (total of max 4) -->
```

```
  (set: _planets to (range: 0, (random: 1, 3) ) )

  <!-- Reset system -->
  (set: $system to (a:) )

  <!-- Create a new system based on the previous random range -->
  (for: each _i, ..._planets )[
    <!-- Add to the new system, setting either RED or GREEN planets -->
    (set: $system to it + (a: (either: "RED", "GREEN") ) )
  ]
}

:: HUD
Health: $health
Fuel: $fuel
Number of Jumps Left: $numberOfJumpsLeft
(display: "Check Status")

:: Display System
{
  (for: each _planet, ...$system)[
    (if: _planet is "RED")[
      (link: _planet)[
        (display: "Show Outcome - Red")
      ]
    ]
    (if: _planet is "GREEN")[
      (link: _planet)[
        (display: "Show Outcome - Green")
      ]
    ]
    <br>
  ]
}

:: Explore Space 1
(link: "Hyperjump")[
  (set: $fuel to it - 1)
  (set: $numberOfJumpsLeft to it - 1)
```

```
    (goto: "Explore Space 2")
]
[(display: "HUD")]<HUD|
(display: "Generate System")
(display: "Display System")

:: Show Outcome - Green
{
   (set: _percentage to (random: 1, 10) )

   (if: _percentage is 1)[

      (set: _foundFuel to (random: 1, 2) )

      Fuel was found in some wreckage. (+_foundFuel to fuel)
      (set: $fuel to it + _foundFuel)

   ] (else-if: _percentage is >= 6)[

      (set: _foundHealth to (random: 1, 3) )

      During a brief pause, the ship was able to be repaired. (+_foundHealth to health)

      (set: $health to it + _foundHealth )

   ] (else:) [
      Nothing happened.
   ]

   (replace: ?HUD)[(display: "HUD")]
}

:: Show Outcome - Red
{
   (set: _percentage to (random: 1, 10) )

   (if: _percentage is >= 6)[

      (set: _foundHealth to (random: 1, 5) )
```

```
    (set: _foundFuel to (random: 1, 3) )

    The hostile environment damaged the ship, but extra fuel was found. (-_foundHealth to
health and +_foundFuel to fuel)

    (set: $health to it - _foundHealth )
    (set: $fuel to it + _foundFuel )

  ] (else-if: _percentage <= 3)[

    (set: _foundHealth to (random: 2, 7) )

    A hostile ship attacked. (-_foundHealth to health)

    (set: $health to it - _foundHealth )

  ] (else:)[
    Nothing happened.
  ]

  (replace: ?HUD)[(display: "HUD")]
}

:: Explore Space 2
(link: "Hyperjump")[
  (set: $fuel to it - 1)
  (set: $numberOfJumpsLeft to it - 1)
  (goto: "Explore Space 1")
]
[(display: "HUD")]<HUD|
(display: "Generate System")
(display: "Display System")

:: Check Status
{
  (if: $health <= 0)[
    (goto: "Destroyed")
  ]
  (if: $fuel <= 0)[
```

```
      (goto: "Lost in space")
    ]
    (if: $numberOfJumpsLeft <= 0)[
      (goto: "Safe")
    ]

}

:: Destroyed
The ship exploded in flight.

###Game Over.

:: Lost in space
Without fuel, the ship tumbled and spun in the endless black.

###Game Over

:: Safe
After 10 hyperjumps, the ship left the hazardous area and called for help.

###Success!
```

Static Healthbars

Summary

"Static Healthbars" demonstrates how to write HTML elements that use variable values. In this example, the **(print:)** macro is used to create **<progress>** and **<meter>** elements. A **(text:)** macro is also used to temporarily convert the current Numeric value of the *$health* story variable into a string value.

Twee Code

```
:: StoryTitle
Static Healthbars for Harlowe

:: Start
(set: $health to 80)

Show a healthbar using a Progress element:
(print: '<progress value="' + (text: $health) + '" max="100"></progress>')

Show a healthbar using a Meter element:
(print: '<meter value="' + (text: $health) + '" min="0" max="100"></meter>')
```

Storylets

Summary

Storylets are a different way of approaching nonlinear storytelling. Instead of linking from one passage to another in Twine, storylets are defined by what are called its *requirements* and *content*.

The metaphor of a deck of cards is often useful in understanding storylets. A card is able to be drawn from a deck if its requirements are met. Through defining many cards (passages in Twine) and conditions under which they can be used (their requirements), dynamic storytelling can take place as different arrangements become possible through writing simple rules for each card.

The **(storylet:)** macro defines a passage as a storylet in Harlowe. It should appear as either the first line or as near to the top of the passage as possible. The value used with the **(storylet:)** macro defines if it is "open" or not. Harlowe uses a **when** lambda to define these, and a storylet is considered "open" when its lambda value evaluates to true when comparing two values or variables.

The **(link-storylet:)** macro selects the first open storylet based on a number passed to the macro. To access the fourth open storylet, for example, **(link-storylet: 4)** could be used. If no storylets are open, a third value can be used in the format of **(link-storylet: 4, "No storylets")** where the fourth open storylet would be used or the value "No storylets" shown to the user if no storylets were available when it checked.

In this example, two passages use the **(storylet:)** macro. One, "Joy Ewers" has a requirement of **$type** being equal to "Hookup". The other passage using the **(storylet:)** macro is "Rhys Johns", which has a requirement of **$type** being equal to "Causal Dating". Depending on the value of **$type**, set in the "Start" passage using the **(cycling-link:)** macro, either one or the other will be open and thereby picked by the **(link-storylet:)** macro. Revisiting the "Start" passage allows for changing the value of **$type** and which storylet is open, changing possible navigation through the story.

Twee Code

```
:: StoryTitle
Harlowe: Storylets

:: StoryData
 {
   "ifid": "D709A2F4-0E88-4010-B157-8ADEDDB2DC74",
   "format": "Harlowe",
   "formatVersion": "3.2.1",
   "zoom": "1",
   "start": "1"
}

:: Start {"position":"199,99","size":"100,100"}
You open the app and wait for it to load. You have never liked dating apps, but agreed to try this new one to get your friend to stop bugging you about it

You stare at the prompt on the screen.

//What are you looking for? (Click to change)//
(cycling-link: bind $type, "Hookup", "Casual Dating")

[[Matches]]

:: Matches {"position":"198,299","size":"100,100"}

(link-storylet: 1)

:: Send message? {"position":"407,402","size":"100,100"}
You send a message and close the app for now.

:: Rhys Johns {"position":"705,229","size":"100,100"}
(storylet: when $type is "Casual Dating")

''Name:'' Rhys Johns

''Pronouns:'' He/Him
```

[[Send message?]]

[[Change search?->Start]]

:: Joy Ewers {"position":"432,204","size":"100,100"}
(storylet: when $type is "Hookup")

''Name:'' Joy Ewers

''Pronouns:'' They/Them

[[Send message?]]

[[Change search?->Start]]

Style Markup

Summary

In Harlowe, style markup can take many forms. Covering italics and boldface as basic examples, Harlowe also provides markup for creating alignment and columns as well.

Twee Code

```
:: StoryTitle
Style Markup in Harlowe

:: Start
//Italics//
''Boldface''
~~Strikethrough text~~
*Emphasis*
**Strong emphasis**
Super^^script^^
``[[Escaped double square brackets]]``
#Level 1 heading
##Level 2 heading
###Level 3 heading
####Level 4 heading
#####Level 5 heading
######Level 6 heading
* Bulleted item
    *    Bulleted item 2
  ** Indented bulleted item
0. Numbered item
   0. Numbered item 2
0.0. Indented numbered item
```

```
==>
This is right-aligned
   =><=
This is centered
  <==>
This is justified
<==
This is left-aligned (undoes the above)
===><=
This has margins 3/4 left, 1/4 right
   =><=====
This has margins 1/6 left, 5/6 right.
|==
This is in the leftmost column, which has a right margin of about 2 letters wide.
    =|||=
This is in the next column, which has margins of 1 letter wide. It is three times as wide as the left column.
  =====||
This is in the right column, which has a right margin of about 5 letters wide. It is twice as wide as the left column.
   |==|
This text is not in columns, but takes up the entire width, as usual.
```

Timed Passages

Summary

Made famous in *Queers in Love at the End of the World* (2013), "Timed Passages" uses the the **(live:)** macro to count seconds while checking if a timer has reached zero. If so, the **(goto:)** macro will immediately move the player to another passage.

Twee Code

```
:: StoryTitle
Harlowe: Timed Passages

:: StoryStylesheet[stylesheet]
tw-include[type="startup"]{
  display: none;
}
tw-sidebar {
    display:none;
}


:: Start
[[Start Timer|First Passage]]

:: World End
The world ended.

:: First Passage
(display: "Timer")

[[Second Passage]]
```

```
:: Timer
{
  (live: 1s)[
      (if: $timer is 0)[
      (stop:)
      (goto: "World End")
    ]
      (else: )[
      (set: $timer to it - 1)
      The world will end in $timer seconds
    ]
  ]
}

:: Second Passage
(display: "Timer")

[[First Passage]]

:: Startup[startup]
(set: $timer to 10)
```

See Also

Harlowe: Delayed Text (pg. 136), Typewritter Effect (pg. 191)

Turn Counter

Summary

"Turn Counter" demonstrates the use of the **(history:)** macro in keeping track of "turns" (number of passages visited).

In this example, the *length* of the array returned by using the **(history:)** macro is compared to its modulo 24 value. Sometimes known as "wrap around," the modulus operator (%) is used to get the remainder of the number of "turns" (passages) divided by 24. This creates a clock where its value shows one of a series of strings representing "morning", "mid-morning", "afternoon", or "night."

By visiting other passages, the turn count is increased and the hour reaches 23 before being reset back to 0 before increasing again.

Twee Code

```
:: StoryTitle
Turn Counter in Harlowe

:: Start
Rooms:
[[Back Room]]
[[Left Room]]
[[Right Room]]

:: Turn Counter[header]
{
  (set: $hour to (history:)'s length % 24 )
  (if: $hour <= 8)[It is morning.]
  (if: $hour > 8 and $hour <= 12)[It is mid-morning.]
  (if: $hour > 12 and $hour <= 16)[It is afternoon.]
  (if: $hour > 16)[It is night.]
}

:: Back Room
Rooms:
```

```
[[Left Room]]
[[Right Room]]
[[Front Room|Start]]

:: Left Room
Rooms:
[[Right Room]]
[[Back Room]]
[[Front Room|Start]]

:: Right Room
Rooms:
[[Left Room]]
[[Back Room]]
[[Front Room|Start]]
```

Typewriter Effect

> **Information**
> This code can only be used once per passage. Additional Harlowe code will not be re-run.

Summary

"Typewriter Effect" demonstrates how to create a delayed character-by-character effect. In Harlowe, this is achieved using the *(live:)* macro to show text on a delay and the *(append:)* macro to append text to a hook.

Twee Code

```
:: StoryTitle
Typewriter Effect in Harlowe

:: Start
<!-- Set the text to show -->
(set: $typewriterText to "Hello, world!")
<!-- Display (call) the Typewriter passage -->
(display: "Typewriter")

:: Typewriter
{
  <!-- Create a variable to track the position within the $typewriterText string -->
  (set: $typewriterPos to 1)

  <!-- Create a hook to hold the typed text -->
  |typewriterOutput>[]

  <!-- Set a delay of 20ms seconds per loop -->
  (live: 20ms)[

    <!-- Add the next character to the hook -->
```

```
    (append: ?typewriterOutput)[(print: $typewriterText's $typewriterPos)]

    <!-- Update the position -->
    (set: $typewriterPos to it + 1)

    <!-- If it's gone past the end, stop -->
    (if: $typewriterPos is $typewriterText's length + 1)[
      (stop:)
    ]
  ]
}
```

See Also

Harlowe: Delayed Text (pg. 136)

Variable Story Styling

Summary

"Variable Story Styling" demonstrates how to combine the **(background:)** and **(color:)** macros and store them in a variable. Using the **(enchant:)** macro, the named hook **?Page** is used to select the entire page and apply the background and color changes in each passage.

Twee Code

```
:: StoryTitle
Variable Story Styling in Harlowe

:: Start
(set: $storyStyle to (background: white) + (color: green) )
(enchant: ?Page, $storyStyle)
This text is green on a white background.
[[Next Passage]]

:: Next Passage
(set: $storyStyle to (background: black) + (color: white) )
(enchant: ?Page, $storyStyle)
This text is white on a black background.
```

```
(link: 'Okay')[ (goto: (history:)'s last) ]

:: dart trap
Several darts shoot out of a wall at you!
<!-- we can check to see if the player has a given item with the contains operator -->
(if: $inventory contains 'a shield')[\
    Luckily, your shield will protect you.
](else:)[\
    With no way to defend yourself, you die.
]
```

Twine 2 Examples: Snowman

Snowman

Adding Functionality

Summary

Snowman does not provide macros. However, additional functionality can be added through the use of the Underscore.js JavaScript library provided with Snowman.

In this example, a global function, *showCurrentTime()*, is added to the *window.setup* object. It is called in a passage through using the interpolation functionality of Underscore's template system to show a value.

Twee Code

```
:: StoryTitle
Adding Functionality in Snowman

:: UserScript[script]
// Use or create window.setup
window.setup = window.setup || {};

// Create global function
window.setup.showCurrentTime = function() {
  return new Date();
}

:: Start
The current time is <%= setup.showCurrentTime() %>
```

Arrays

Summary

Arrays are a collection of values. Each value in an array is assigned an *index*, which is a number that corresponds to the position of that item or element in the array. In JavaScript, arrays are *zero-based*, meaning the first element in the array is given the index "0". Arrays have many built-in methods and other features for your use. You can create an array by assigning a variable to the array literal, which is a pair of brackets ([]): `<% s.myArray = [] %>`.

Specific elements can be accessed in an array by following its variable name with a pair of brackets containing the index to check. Testing whether an array contains an element can be done using the **Array#includes()** function; adding new items can be done using the **Array#push()** function.

Twee Code

```
:: StoryTitle
Arrays in Snowman

:: UserScript [script]
(function () {
    var s = window.story.state;
    s.inventory = [];
    s.chest = ['a shield', 'a suit of armor'];
    s.chestOpen = false;
}());

:: Header
You are currently carrying:
<% if (s.inventory.length === 0) { %>
nothing.
<% } else { %>
<%= s.inventory.join(', ') + '.' %>
<% } %>
```

```
:: Start
<%= window.story.render("Header") %><hr />

You find yourself inside a small room. In the corner, you see a sword, and decide to
pick it up.

<% s.inventory.push('a sword') %>
[[Continue|hallway]]

:: hallway
<%= window.story.render("Header") %><hr />
You see a chest here in the hallway.
<% if (!s.chestOpen) { %>
Do you want to open it?

[[Open the chest.|chest]]
<% } else { %>
It's open, and there's nothing inside.
<% } %>

[[Move on.|dart trap]]

:: chest
<% s.inventory = s.inventory.concat(s.chest) %>
<% s.chestOpen = true %>
<%= window.story.render("Header") %><hr />

You open the chest and find <%= s.chest.join(' and ') %>.

[[Okay.|hallway]]

:: dart trap
<%= window.story.render("Header") %><hr />
Several darts shoot out of a wall at you!
<% if (s.inventory.includes('a shield')) { %>

Luckily, your shield will protect you.
<% } else { %>

With no way to defend yourself, you die.
<% } %>
```

Audio

> **Information**
> This examples uses two additional files, **testpattern.ogg** and **testpattern.wav**. Both files need to be downloaded from the online Cookbook and placed in the same folder as the HTML file in order to work as designed.

Summary

Snowman does not have direct macro support for audio resources. However, additional JavaScript can be added to work with audio elements within a story.

Audio elements rely on sources either absolutely or relatively located. An absolute reference starts with HTTP or another protocol; a relative reference describes the location of the resource in relation to the webpage. Because audio files are external resources, they must also be accessed from a remote service, file hosting location, or stored separately with the webpage.

Due to browser differences in licensing, some audio formats are not universally supported. For best results in using audio in Twine, it is recommended to use multiple formats, allowing the browser to choose which one is best supported when first loaded.

Twee Code

```
:: StoryTitle
Audio in Snowman

:: Start
<audio controls>
  <source src="testpattern.ogg" type="audio/ogg">
  <source src="testpattern.wav" type="audio/wav">
Your browser does not support the audio element.
</audio>
```

Conditional Statements

Summary

Through using the *s* global variable and the built-in Underscore template functionality, JavaScript conditional statements can be run to show content in Snowman.

Twee Code

```
:: StoryTitle
Conditional Statements in Snowman

:: Start
<%
  s.animal = "horse";
%>

<% if(s.animal == "dog"){ %>
It's a dog!
<% } else { %>
It's a horse!
<% } %>
```

See Also

> **Snowman: Setting and Showing Variables (pg. 257)**

CSS Selectors

Summary

This example shows how to use CSS selectors to style different areas of the page. Snowman 2.0 uses the elements **<tw-story>** and **<tw-passage>** to show a passage. It also changes from an *id* to a *class* named "passage" from previous versions of Snowman.

```
<body>
  <tw-story>
    <tw-passage class="passage"></tw-passage>
  </tw-story>
</body>
```

Twee Code

```
:: StoryTitle
CSS Selectors in Snowman

:: UserStylesheet [stylesheet]
body {
    background-color: lightgreen;
}

tw-passage {
    border: 1px solid red;
}

:: Start
The page has a green background; it contains this passage, which has a red border.

[[Second]]
```

```
:: Second
This passage also has a red border.
```

See Also

Styling passages using the id CSS selector
Snowman: Left Sidebar (pg. 229)

CSS and Passage Tags

Summary

This example shows how to use CSS selectors to style different passages. Snowman does not support tags in passages. However, the effect can be implemented through using jQuery and the **toggleClass()** function to switch between different pre-defined classes.

Twee Code

```
:: StoryTitle
CSS and Passage Tags in Snowman

:: UserStylesheet[stylesheet]
.grey {
  background: grey;
  color: white;
}
.yellow {
  background: yellow;
  color: black;
}

:: Start[grey]
<% $("body").toggleClass("grey") %>
This passage has a grey background and white text.

[[Second]]

:: Second[yellow]
<% $("body").toggleClass("yellow") %>
This passage has a yellow background and black text.
```

Cycling Choices

Summary

"Cycling Choices" demonstrates how to create a link which cycles through different choices when clicked on.

Starting with iterating over all elements with the class **.cycle**, each element's "choices" and "selection" attribute values are saved as global variables. They are not expected to change during the story. Next, by using jQuery, a *.click()* trigger is set for all elements with the class **.cycle**.

When triggered, the global values of "choices" and "selection" for the element are retrieved and the "selection" attribute is updated. The **text()** of the element is set to the "selection" index of the "choices"* array.

Finally, the global variables are updated according to the element's *id* for later access and to prevent changes to the history of the story potentially affecting saved values.

Twee Code

```
:: StoryTitle
Cycling Choices in Snowman

:: UserScript[script]
$(function() {

  // Create a global object
  window.setup = window.setup || {};

  // Iterate through all elements with the class 'cycle'
  //   For each, save the current 'choices' and 'selection'
  //   (This sets all the 'default' values.)
  $('.cycle').each(function() {
```

```javascript
  // Create a global object for each 'id'
  var id = $(this).attr('id');
  setup[id] = {};

  // Save the current 'choices' for each
  var choices = JSON.parse($(this).attr("data-cycling-choices"));
  setup[id].choices = choices;

  // Save the current 'selection' for each
  var selection = $(this).attr("data-cycling-selection");
  setup[id].selection = selection;

});

$('.cycle').click(function(){

  // Save the 'id'
  var id = $(this).attr('id');

  // Retrieve the global 'choices'
  var choices = setup[id].choices;

  // Retrieve the global 'selection'
  var selection = setup[id].selection;

  // Update the 'selection' number
  selection++;

  // Check if 'selection' is greater than length of choices
  if(selection >= choices.length) {
    selection = 0;
  }

  // Update the 'selection' on the element
  $(this).attr("data-cycling-selection", selection);

  // Update the text of the element with the choice
  $(this).text(choices[selection]);
```

```
        // Update the global values of 'choices' and 'selection'
        setup[id].choices = choices;
        setup[id].selection = selection;

    });

});

:: Start
<a href='javascript:void(0)' id='cycleOne' class='cycle' data-cycling-choices='["One", "Two", "Three"]' data-cycling-selection=0>One</a>

[[Submit|Results]]

:: Results
<%= setup["cycleOne"].choices[setup["cycleOne"].selection] %>
```

See Also

Snowman: Setting and Showing Variables (pg. 257)

Date and Time

Summary

"Date and Time" demonstrates how to use the JavaScript *Date()* functionality in Snowman.

Twee Code

```
:: StoryTitle
Date and Time in Snowman

:: Start
The current time (in milliseconds since January 1, 1970 00:00:00 UTC) is <%= Date.now() %>

<%
  window.setup = {};
  window.setup.newDate = new Date();
%>
The current month is <%= setup.newDate.getMonth() %>.

The current day is <%= setup.newDate.getDay() %>.

The current hour is <%= setup.newDate.getHours() %>.

The current minute is <%= setup.newDate.getMinutes() %>.

The current fullyear is <%= setup.newDate.getFullYear() %>.

<% window.setup.originalDate = new Date("October 20, 2018") %>
It has been <%=  Date.now() - setup.originalDate%> milliseconds since October 20, 2018.
```

Delayed Text

Summary

"Delayed Text" uses the **delay()** function in Underscore combined with a jQuery selector to target an element with the *id* of "results" to change its internal text after five seconds.

Twee Code

```
:: StoryTitle
Delayed Text in Snowman

:: Start
<div id="results"></div>
<%
 _.delay(
  function() {
    $("#results").text("It has been 5 seconds. Show the text!");
  },
  5000);
%>
```

See Also

Snowman: Typewriter Effect (pg. 278)

Deleting Variables

Summary

Through using the Underscore template library available in Snowman, JavaScript can be used within passages without a **<script>** tag. The **delete** operator can be used in JavaScript to remove a variable.

Twee Code

```
:: StoryTitle
Snowman: Deleting Variables

:: UserScript[script]
window.story = {};

window.story.example = "an example!";

:: Start
What is the value of the property "example" of the object window.story? <%= window.story.example %>

[[Delete the value!]]

:: Delete the value!
<%

// Delete the variable
delete window.story.example;

%>

[[Test for value]]

:: Test for value
Does "example" still exist as part of the object window.story? <%= window.story.hasOwnProperty("example") %>
```

Dice Rolling

Summary

"Dice Rolling" demonstrates how to create the same effects of rolling various physical dice through using Underscore.js's **_.random()** function and its interpolating functionality.

Twee Code

```
:: StoryTitle
Snowman: Dice Rolling

:: Start
Rolling a 1d4: <%= _.random(1,4) %>

Rolling a 1d6: <%= _.random(1,6) %>

Rolling a 1d8: <%= _.random(1,8) %>

Rolling a 1d10: <%= _.random(1, 10) %>

Rolling a 1d12: <%= _.random(1, 12) %>

Rolling a 1d20: <%= _.random(1, 20) %>

Rolling a 1d100: <%= _.random(1, 100) %>

Rolling a 1d4 + 4: <%= _.random(1, 4) + 4 %>

Rolling a 1d6 - 2: <%= _.random(1, 6) - 2 %>

Rolling a 2d6 + 10: <%= _.random(1, 6) + _.random(1, 6) + 10 %>
```

```
Rolling a 1d4 + 4: {_example1}

Rolling a 1d6 - 2: {_example2}

Rolling a 2d6 + 10: {_example3}
```

Fairmath System

Summary

"Fairmath System" demonstrates how to re-create the Fairmath system found in ChoiceScript. Based on a percentage operation, increase and decrease changes the value by a percentage as the difference between the original and adjusted value.

This example uses functions **increase()** and **decrease()** as part of a created global *window.setup.fairmath*. These can be called through using the Underscore template functionality to define, use, and show the values of the functions in any one passage.

Twee Code

```
:: StoryTitle
Fairmath in Snowman

:: UserScript[script]
// Create a global object
window.setup = window.setup || {};

// Create a fairmath global object
window.setup.fairmath = {};

// Create an 'increase' function
setup.fairmath.increase = function(x,y) {
   return Math.round(x+((100-x)*(y/100)));
};

// Create a "decrease" function
setup.fairmath.decrease = function(x,y) {
   return Math.round(x-(x*(y/100)));
};

:: Start
```

```
Decrease 100 by 50% using Fairmath:
<%= setup.fairmath.decrease(100, 50) %>

Increase 50 by 50% using Fairmath:
<%= setup.fairmath.increase(50, 50) %>
```

Geolocation

Summary

Many browsers allow access to the user's current location through the Geolocation property and associated functions. This functionality is subject to the user agreeing to allow access. Until the functionality is unlocked, or if the user declines, default values will be returned.

Functionality availability and their results should always be tested against other location services or information. Most browsers will return results through the fastest and sometimes least-accurate methods possible.

This example uses Underscore template functionality to test for and show the values of properties storied in the *s* global variable in Snowman.

Twee Code

```
:: StoryTitle
Geolocation in Snowman

:: UserScript[script]
(function () {

  window.geolocation = {

    available: function() {
      return ("geolocation" in navigator
        && typeof navigator.geolocation.getCurrentPosition === "function");
    },
    getLocation: function() {

      // Create initial values
      var location = { latitude : 0, longitude : 0 };
```

```javascript
    // Create success callback to store values
    var  positionSuccess = function (position) {

      location.latitude = position.coords.latitude;
      location.longitude = position.coords.longitude;

    };

    // Create error callback
    var positionError = function (error) {
      /* Code that handles errors */
    };

    // Create initial options
    var positionOptions = {
      timeout: 31000,
      enableHighAccuracy: true,
      maximumAge : 120000
    };


    // Ask for location based on callbacks and options
    navigator.geolocation.getCurrentPosition(
      positionSuccess,
      positionError,
      positionOptions
    );

    // Return location found
    // If not location, will return initial (0,0) values
    return location;

},
approximateLocation: function (a, b, allowedDiff) {
    // allowedDiff must always be > 0
  if (a === b) { // handles various "exact" edge cases
    return true;
  }
```

```
      allowedDiff = allowedDiff || 0.0005;

      return Math.abs(a - b) < allowedDiff;
    }

  };

}());

:: Start
[[Ask for permission]]

:: Show results
Is geolocation available? <%= window.geolocation.available() %>
<%
  if(window.geolocation.available()) {
    s.location = window.geolocation.getLocation();
  }
%>

If so, what is the current location?

Latitude: <%= s.location.latitude %>

Longitude: <%= s.location.longitude %>

Are we in the approximate location of Stonehenge (51.1788853, -1.828409)?

Latitude: <%= window.geolocation.approximateLocation(s.location.latitude, 51.1788853) %>

Longitude: <%= window.geolocation.approximateLocation(s.location.longitude, -1.828409) %>

:: Ask for permission
<%
  if(window.geolocation.available()) {
    s.location = window.geolocation.getLocation();
  }
%>
[[Show results]]
```

Google Fonts

Summary

"Google Fonts" uses a Google Font loaded via the CSS **@import** at-rule. A class style rule ("message") is then created using the imported font-family and applied to a **<div>** element within a single passage.

Other Google Fonts could be imported and applied using the same method, creating new class or ID style rules to be applied for and across different HTML elements in the same way.

Twee Code

```
:: StoryTitle
Snowman: Google Fonts

:: StoryStylesheet[stylesheet]
@import url('https://fonts.googleapis.com/css?family=Roboto');

.message {
  font-family: 'Roboto', sans-serif;
}

:: Start
<div class="message">This text is styled using a Google Font</div>
```

Headers and Footers

Summary

"Headers and Footers" demonstrates the use of the **window.story.render()** function to return the HTML contents of another passage. Combined with Underscore template functionality, the content of passages can be "displayed" in others. Because Snowman does not have pre-defined 'header' or 'footer' functionality, using these two different methods together can create the same result. However, the code would need to be included on any additional passages to continue the effect.

Twee Code

```
:: StoryTitle
Snowman: Headers and Footers

:: Start
<%= window.story.render("Header") %>

This content is between the header and the footer.

<%= window.story.render("Footer") %>

:: Header
This is the header!

:: Footer
This is the footer!
```

See Also

Snowman: Passage Events (pg. 243)

Hidden Link

Summary

"Hidden Link" demonstrates how to create a 'hidden' link that is only revealed when the cursor passes over it.

Using CSS and JavaScript, a rule is created for transparent color and applied or removed through using jQuery's **on()** function with 'mouseenter' and 'mouseleave' events.

Twee Code

```
:: StoryTitle
Snowman: Hidden Link

:: UserScript[script]
$(function () {
  /*
    Hidden links that are always hidden:
      <span class="hidden">[[A hidden link]]</span>
  */
  $('.hidden')
    .addClass('hidden');

  /*
    Hidden links that hide unless you're hovering over them:
      <span class="hides">[[A hidden link]]</span>
  */
  $('.hides')
    .addClass('hidden')
    .on('mouseenter', function () {
      $(this).removeClass('hidden');
    })
    .on('mouseleave', function () {
      $(this).addClass('hidden');
    });
```

```
	/*
		Hidden links that reveal themselves when you hover over them:
			<span class="reveals">[[A hidden link]]</span>
	*/
	$('.reveals')
		.addClass('hidden')
		.one('mouseenter', function () {
			$(this).removeClass('hidden');
		});
});

:: UserStylesheet[stylesheet]
.hidden a {
	color: transparent;
		/* By default links in Snowman have a border */
		border-bottom: 0px;
}


:: Start
A hidden link that's always hidden: <span class="hidden">[[A hidden link]]</span>

A hidden link that hides unless you're hovering over it: <span class="hides">[[A hidden link]]</span>

A hidden link that reveals itself when you hover over it: <span class="reveals">[[A hidden link]]</span>


:: A hidden link
You found it!
```

Images

Summary

When using Snowman, images can be displayed through the image HTML element and **url()** CSS data type when encoded as Base64.

When using an image element, its source is either absolutely or relatively located. An absolute reference starts with HTTP or another protocol; a relative reference describes the location of the image in relation to the webpage.

Because images are external resources, they need to be included with the webpage as Base64-encoded or in another location. While Base64-encoded images can be embedded in a webpage, it also increases its overall size. External images require additional hosting and are included through their reference in CSS (URL) data type or image (SRC) attribute.

Twee Code

```
:: StoryTitle
Images in Snowman

:: UserStylesheet[stylesheet]
.base64image {
  width: 256px;
  height: 256px;
  /* Base64 image truncated for example */
  /* See Twee file for full version. */
  background-image: url('data:image/png;base64...');
}

:: Start
This is an image element:

<img src="https://twinery.org/homepage/img/logo.svg" width="256" height="256">
```

This is a Base64-encoded CSS image background:

<div class="base64image"></div>

Importing External JavaScript

> **Information**
> The successful loading of an external JavaScript file or library commonly produces no visual output. The code within the example passage is not required for the successful loading of an external file or library.

Summary

"Importing External JavaScript" demonstrates how to import an externally stored JavaScript library, jQuery UI.

This example uses the built-in jQuery **$.getScript()** function to load the library and demonstrates a short example of how to use it.

Twee Code

```
:: StoryTitle
Snowman: Importing External JavaScript


:: UserScript [script]
/* import jQuery UI library. */
$(function () {
  $.getScript("https://ajax.googleapis.com/ajax/libs/jqueryui/1.12.1/jquery-ui.min.js",
    function (data, textStatus, jqxhr) {
      console.log('jquery ui file loaded');
    }
  );
});
```

:: Start
```
<p>Click on the grey box below to see it bounce.</p>
<div id="box" style="width: 100px; height: 100px; background: #ccc;"></div>

<script>
$("#box").click(function () {
  $("#box").toggle("bounce", {times: 3}, "slow");
});
</script>
```

Keyboard Events

Summary

"Keyboard Events" demonstrates how to capture keyboard events and then how to associate individual keys with activities within a story.

The example uses jQuery's **on()** function to monitor for all "keyup" events. Once a "keyup" event has occurred, two values are available:

- The *keyCode* property: the numerical value representing the key presented in its decimal ASCII code supported by effectively all browsers.
- The *key* property: the string value of the key presented supported by most modern web-browsers.

Twee Code

```
:: StoryTitle
Snowman: Keyboard


:: UserScript[script]
(function () {
  $(document).on('keyup', function (ev) {
    /* the ev variable contains a keyup event object.
     *
     * ev.keyCode - contains the ASCII code of the key that was released, this property is supported in effectively all browsers.
     * ev.key     - contains the key value of the key that was released, this property is supported by most modern browsers.
     *
     */


    /* the following shows an alert when the 'a' key is released. */
```

```
    if (ev.key === 'a') {
      alert("the 'a' key was released.");
    }
  });
}());
```

:: Start
Press and release the "a" key to show an Alert dialog.

Left Sidebar

Summary

Snowman does not have a built-in sidebar, but one can be created using JavaScript, jQuery, and CSS.

The **createElement()** function is used to create a new **<div>** element where the generated output of the Sidebar passage will be added. This new **<div>** is assigned an ID of "sidebar" using the **attr()** function and then inserted into the story's Document Object Model (DOM) using the **insertBefore()** function.

Snowman triggers a **showpassage:after** event after each passage is shown. The **on()** function can be used to monitor for this event. Once the event has occurred, a combination of the **html()** and **window.story.render()** functions can be used to display the dynamic contents of the Sidebar passage within the "sidebar" **<div>** element.

Twee Code

```
:: StoryTitle
Left Sidebar in Snowman


:: UserScript [script]
/*
    Create the element to display the contents of the Sidebar passage in.
*/
$(document.createElement('div'))
    .attr('id', 'sidebar')
    .insertBefore('.passage');

/*
    Monitor for the event that is triggered after the current Passage has been shown.
*/
```

```
$(window).on('hide.sm.passage', function () {
    $('#sidebar').html(window.story.render("sidebar"));
});


:: UserStylesheet[stylesheet]
.passage {
  margin-left: 20%;
}

#sidebar {
  position: fixed;
  top: 0;
  left: 0;
  width: 18%;
  height: 100%;
  margin: 0;
  padding: 0.5em;
  background-color: black;
  color: white;
}


:: Start
<% s.name = "Jane Doe"; s.location = "Work" %>
[[Another passage]]


:: Sidebar
Name: <%= s.name %><br>
Location: <%= s.location %>


:: Another passage
<% s.name = "John Smith"; s.location = "Shop" %>
[[Start]]
```

Lock and Key: Variable

Summary

"Lock and Key: Variable" demonstrates how to create the effect of picking up a key and unlocking a door. In this example, the key is a variable (*s.key*) and does not initially exist in the Start passage.

When the link "Pick up the key" is clicked, *s.key* is changed to the value "true" and the door link changes from its initial response of "Locked Door" to a link to the passage Exit.

Twee Code

```
:: StoryTitle
Lock and Key: Variable in Snowman

:: Start
Rooms:
- [[Front Room]]
- [[Back Room]]

:: Front Room
<% if (s.key) { %>
[[Exit]]
<% } else { %>
*Locked Door*
<% } %>

Rooms:
- [[Back Room]]

:: Back Room
<% if (!s.key) { %>
Items:
- <a href="javascript:void(0)" class="key-item">Pick up key</a>
```

```
<% } else { %>
There is nothing here.
<% } %>

<%
$(function() {
  $('.key-item').click(function() {
    s.key = true;
    $(this).replaceWith('<span>You have a key.</span>');
  });
});
%>

Rooms:
- [[Front Room]]

:: Exit
You found the key and went through the door!
```

See Also

Snowman: Setting and Showing Variables (pg. 257)

Looping

Summary

In programming terminology, a "loop" is a common technique for iterating (moving through one by one) some type of data. Because Snowman does not provide macros, the existing JavaScript **for** keyword can be used to create loops. Since Snowman also includes the Underscore.js and jQuery libraries, the **_.each()** and **jQuery.each()** functions can also be used.

In this example, the *s* global shortcut to the *window.story.state* variable used. A new property called "arrayInventory" is set to the series of values "Bread", "Pan", and "Book". The first example uses the JavaScript **for** keyword to move through the values. The second example uses the **_.each()** function in Underscore.js, and the third uses the **jQuery.each()** function for the same purpose.

Twee Code

```
:: StoryTitle
Looping in Snowman

:: Start
<%
// An array of the strings "Bread", "Pan", "Book"
s.arrayInventory = ["Bread", "Pan", "Book"];

// An example using JavaScript
for (var i = 0; i < s.arrayInventory.length; i++){
 %>You have <%= s.arrayInventory[i] %>.<br> <%
}
%>

<hr>
<%
// An example using Underscore.js
_.each(s.arrayInventory, function(item) {
```

```
    %>You have <%= item %>.<br> <%
});
%>


<hr>
<%
// An example using jQuery
jQuery.each(s.arrayInventory, function( index, value ) {
    %>You have <%= value %>.<br> <%
});

%>
```

Modal (Pop-up Window)

Summary

This example uses the jQuery **click()** and **show()/hide()** functions to watch for the user clicking on a button (to open) or "X" (to close). Additional CSS rules are used to create the effect of having the content 'behind' the modal window be darkened and unusable until the modal itself is closed.

Twee Code

```
:: StoryTitle
Snowman: Modal

:: UserScript[script]
$(function(){

    // When the user clicks the button, open the modal
    $("#myBtn").click(function() {
        $("#myModal").show();
    });

    // When the user clicks on <span> (x), close the modal
    $(".close").click(function() {
        $("#myModal").hide();
    });

});


:: UserStylesheet[stylesheet]
/* The Modal (background) */
.modal {
    display: none; /* Hidden by default */
    position: fixed; /* Stay in place */
```

```css
    z-index: 1; /* Sit on top */
    padding-top: 100px; /* Location of the box */
    left: 0;
    top: 0;
    width: 100%; /* Full width */
    height: 100%; /* Full height */
    overflow: auto; /* Enable scroll if needed */
    background-color: rgb(0,0,0); /* Fallback color */
    background-color: rgba(0,0,0,0.4); /* Black w/ opacity */
}

/* Modal Content */
.modal-content {
    background-color: #fefefe;
    margin: auto;
    padding: 20px;
    border: 1px solid #888;
    width: 80%;
}

/* The Close Button */
.close {
    color: #aaaaaa;
    float: right;
    font-size: 28px;
    font-weight: bold;
}

.close:hover,
.close:focus {
    color: #000;
    text-decoration: none;
    cursor: pointer;
}
```

```
:: Start
<button id="myBtn">Open Modal</button>

<div id="myModal" class="modal">
  <div class="modal-content">
    <span class="close">×</span>
    <p>Example text in the modal</p>
  </div>
</div>
```

Modularity

Summary

In programming terminology, modularity refers to dividing software into different sections related to their purpose or to better organize the whole. In Snowman, this technique can be used through the **window.story.render()** function to print the contents of one passage in another. Parts of a story can often be re-used in this way.

Twee Code

```
:: StoryTitle
Modularity in Snowman

:: Start
<%
  s.lineOne = "Give us a verse";
  s.lineTwo = "Drop some knowledge";
%>

<%= window.story.render("showLineOne") %>
<%= window.story.render("showLineTwo") %>


:: showLineOne
<%= s.lineOne %>

:: showLineTwo
<%= s.lineTwo %>
```

Moving through a dungeon

Summary

"Moving through a 'dungeon'" creates a multidimensional array. Movement positions are then tracked through X and Y variables for a grid system. Each movement subtracts or adds to its corresponding X or Y position and is compared to those same positions within the array. Different directions are shown if movement is possible in that direction.

Twee Code

```
:: StoryTitle
Snowman: Moving through Dungeons

:: User Style [stylesheet]
.passage{
   font-family:monospace;
}

:: Start
<div class="maze"></div>

<button type="button" data-move="n">North</button>
<button type="button" data-move="s">South</button>
<button type="button" data-move="e">East</button>
<button type="button" data-move="w">West</button>

<%
/* 0s are walls, 1 are spaces, 2 is the goal. */
var maze =
[
[0,0,0,0,0,0,0,0,0,0,0],
[0,1,1,1,0,1,1,1,1,1,0],
[0,0,0,1,0,0,0,0,0,1,0],
[0,1,0,1,1,1,1,1,0,1,0],
```

```
    [0,1,0,0,0,0,0,1,0,1,0],
    [0,1,1,1,1,1,1,1,0,1,0],
    [0,0,0,0,0,0,0,1,0,1,0],
    [0,1,0,1,1,1,1,1,1,1,0],
    [0,1,0,1,0,0,0,1,0,0,0],
    [0,1,1,1,0,1,1,1,1,2,0],
    [0,0,0,0,0,0,0,0,0,0,0]
];

/* Where the player starts. The top left is (0, 0). */

var positionX = 1, positionY = 1;

function renderMaze() {
  /* Transform the maze into ASCII art. */

  /* What characters we use to display the maze. */
  var displayChars = ['#', '.', 'E'];

  $('.maze').html(maze.map(function(row, renderY) {
    return row.reduceRight(function(html, cell, renderX) {
      if (renderX === positionX && renderY === positionY) {
        return 'P' + html;
      }

      return displayChars[cell] + html;
    }, '<br>');
  }));
}

function updateMoves() {
  /*
  Enable/disable buttons to move based on what's allowed.
  We take advantage of the fact that both 0 and undefined
  (outside the maze) are converted to false by JavaScript by the
  ! operator.
  */

  $('[data-move="n"]').attr('disabled', !maze[positionY - 1][positionX]);
```

```
    $('[data-move="s"]').attr('disabled', !maze[positionY + 1][positionX]);
    $('[data-move="e"]').attr('disabled', !maze[positionY][positionX + 1]);
    $('[data-move="w"]').attr('disabled', !maze[positionY][positionX - 1]);
}

$(function() {
  renderMaze();
  updateMoves();

  /*
  Change position when the user clicks an appropriate link.
  We depend on updateMoves() to prevent the user from walking
  through a wall.
  */

  $('[data-move]').click(function() {
    var direction = $(this).data('move');

    switch (direction) {
      case 'n':
        positionY--;
        break;
      case 's':
        positionY++;
        break;
      case 'e':
        positionX++;
        break;
      case 'w':
        positionX--;
        break;
      default:
        throw new Error('Don\'t know how to move ' + direction);
    }

    if (maze[positionY][positionX] === 2) {
      story.show('Exit');
    }
    else {
```

```
      renderMaze();
      updateMoves();
    }
  });
});

%>
```

:: Exit
You've escaped this fiendish maze!

See Also

Snowman: Conditional Statements (pg. 201), Setting and Showing Variables (pg. 257)

Passage Events

Summary

Snowman triggers different events as they happen to passages.

In this example, a header and footer are created by listening for the 'shown.sm.passage' event with a jQuery event handle. These passages are then prepending the content of the passage "Header" and appending the content of the passage "Footer" to the current passage after it has been initially rendered.

Twee Code

```
:: StoryTitle
Snowman: Passage Events

:: UserScript[script]
/*
    Prepend the content of the passage "Header" to every passage.
    Append the content of the passage "Footer" to every passage.
*/
$(window).on('shown.sm.passage', function (eventObject, passageObject) {
    var headerContent = window.story.render("Header");
    var currentContent = passageObject.passage.render();
    var footerContent = window.story.render("Footer");

    $('#main').html(headerContent + currentContent + footerContent);
});

:: Start
[[Another Passage]]

:: Another Passage
[[Back to Beginning|Start]]
```

```
:: Header
This is the header!

:: Footer
This is the footer!
```

See Also

Snowman: Headers and Footers (pg. 218)

Passages in Passages

Summary

In Snowman, the contents of one passage can be included in another passage through use of the *window.story.render()* function. This will find and return the source of an existing passage in the story. Combined with the use of Underscore's template system, the returned value can be included directly where the function is used in a passage.

Twee Code

```
:: StoryTitle
Snowman: Passages in Passages

:: Start
This is the Start passage!
<%= window.story.render("Another") %>

:: Another
And this is Another passage!
```

Render Passage to Element

Summary

In Snowman, the function **renderToSelector()** renders the contents of a passage into an element based on its jQuery selector.

The event "sm.passage.shown" is used in this example to guarantee that the passage has been rendered before acting. Calling the function **renderToSelector()** inside a jQuery event listener then renders another passage into an existing element.

Twee Code

```
:: StoryTitle
Snowman: Render to Element

:: Start
<div id="hudID"></div>
<script>
$(document).one('sm.passage.shown', function (ev) {
  // Render the passage named HUD into the element with id of "hudID"
    renderToSelector("#hudID", "HUD");
  });
</script>

:: HUD
<h1>This is the HUD!</h1>
```

Passage Transitions

Summary

In Snowman 2.X, the **sm.passage.showing** event is triggered once a passage is loaded. By listening for this event, jQuery effects can be applied to the passage element to produce a transition. (In Snowman 2.X, the passage is the **tw-passage** element.)

Twee Code

```
:: StoryTitle
Snowman 2: Passage Transitions

:: UserScript[script]
$(document).on('sm.passage.showing', function(event, passage) {

  $("tw-passage").hide(0).fadeIn(2000);

});

:: Start
[[Another Passage]]

:: Another Passage
[[A Third Passage]]

:: A Third Passage
Double-click this passage to edit it.
```

Passage Visits

Summary

Starting with Snowman 2.0, the global function *visited()* returns the number of times one or more passages have been visited during the course of the story. Combined with the use of Underscore template interpolation, the result of the function can be printed in a passage.

Twee Code

```
:: StoryTitle
Snowman: Passage Visits

:: Start
How many times has the passage "Another Passage" been visited? <%= visited("Another Passage") %>

[[Another Passage]]

:: Another Passage
[[Start]]
```

Player Statistics

> **Information**
> Elements must exist *before* the attempt to bind to them in order to be successful. This example uses the **ready()** function to achieve this with the first, starting passage.

Summary

Some of the most popular mechanics from table-top role-playing games are those where the player must determine their in-game statistics and then use them to make decisions.

In this example, the jQuery event handler **click()** is used to bind multiple buttons. Depending on what was clicked, the content is replaced or the values are adjusted based on if a conditional statement is true. Values are then tested when combined with a random number between 1 to 6, mimicking a common 1d6 mechanic to check if a value is above a target number.

Twee Code

```
:: StoryTitle
Player Statistics in Snowman

:: UserScript[script]
$(function() {

  // Create a global setup object
  window.setup = window.setup || {};

  // Create a global propety on the setup object
  window.setup.stats = {};

  // Create (and overwrite) the use of 's'
  var s = window.setup.stats;

  s.empathy = 10;
```

```
s.intelligence = 10;
s.totalPoints = 5;

$("#empathyIncrease").click(function(){
  if(s.totalPoints > 0) {
    setup.stats.empathy++;
    s.totalPoints--;
    $("#empathyStat").text(s.empathy);
    $("#pointsStat").text(s.totalPoints);
  }
});

$("#empathyDecrease").click(function(){
  if(s.empathy > 0) {
    s.empathy--;
    s.totalPoints++;
    $("#empathyStat").text(s.empathy);
    $("#pointsStat").text(s.totalPoints);
  }
});

$("#intelligenceIncrease").click(function(){
  if(s.totalPoints > 0) {
    s.intelligence++;
    s.totalPoints--;
    $("#intelligenceStat").text(s.intelligence);
    $("#pointsStat").text(s.totalPoints);
  }
});

$("#intelligenceDecrease").click(function(){
  if(s.intelligence > 0) {
    s.intelligence--;
    s.totalPoints++;
    $("#intelligenceStat").text(s.intelligence);
    $("#pointsStat").text(s.totalPoints);
  }
});
```

```
$("#pointsReset").click(function(){
    s.empathy = 10;
    s.intelligence = 10;
    s.totalPoints = 5;
    $("#empathyStat").text(s.empathy);
    $("#intelligenceStat").text(s.intelligence);
    $("#pointsStat").text(s.totalPoints);
});

// Add a randomInt function to the Math global
Math.randomInt = function(min, max) {
   min = Math.ceil(min);
   max = Math.floor(max);
   return Math.floor(Math.random() * (max - min)) + min;
};

$("#testIntelligence").click(function() {

   var result = s.intelligence + Math.randomInt(1,6);

   if(result >= 15) {
      $("#intelligenceResult").text("Success! (" + result + " >= 15)");
   } else {
      $("#intelligenceResult").text("Failure! (" + result + " < 15)");
   }

   console.log("Test!");
});

$("#testEmpathy").click(function() {

   var result = s.empathy + Math.randomInt(1,6);

   if(result >= 15) {
      $("#empathyResult").text("Success! (" + result + " >= 15)");
   } else {
      $("#empathyResult").text("Failure! (" + result + " < 15)");
   }
```

```
    });

});

:: Start
Empathy: <button id="empathyIncrease">[+]</button> <button id="empathyDecrease">[-]</button>

Intelligence: <button id="intelligenceIncrease">[+]</button> <button id="intelligenceDecrease">[-]</button>

<button id="pointsReset">[Reset Points]</button>

Empathy: <span id="empathyStat">10</span>

Intelligence: <span id="intelligenceStat">10</span>

Remaining Points: <span id="pointsStat">5</span>

<button id="testIntelligence">Make an intelligence check?</button>
<div id="intelligenceResult"></div>

<button id="testEmpathy">Make an empathy check?</button>
<div id="empathyResult"></div>
```

See Also

Snowman: Conditional Statements (pg. 205), Setting and Showing Variables (pg. 255)

Programmatic Undo

> **Information**
> Checkpoints will only affect properties of the **s** (state) global variable in Snowman.

Summary

Snowman comes with no user-facing functionality for undoing and re-doing actions. However, by using jQuery and a combination of the **window.story.checkpoint()** and **window.history.back()*** functions, this can be emulated.

Twee Code

```
:: StoryTitle
Programmatic Undo in Snowman

:: UserScript[script]
$(window).on('show.sm.passage', function (e, data)
{
    window.story.checkpoint(data.passage.name);
});

:: Start
[[Enter the Darkness]]

:: Enter the Darkness
<a href="javascript: window.history.back();">You are not ready! Go back!</a>
```

Saving Games

Summary

Snowman provides the **window.story.saveHash()** and **window.story.restore()** functions to produce a hash of the current story state and then recover it. However, it does not provide a mechanism for saving the hash between sessions. Through using the *window.localStorage* global variable, this can be accomplished.

Twee Code

```
:: StoryTitle
Saving Games in Snowman

:: UserScript[script]
window.storage = {
  ok: function() {
    try {
        var storage = window["localStorage"],
          x = '__storage_test__';
        storage.setItem(x, x);
        storage.removeItem(x);
        return true;
    }
    catch(e) {
      return e instanceof DOMException && (
      // everything except Firefox
      e.code === 22 ||
      // Firefox
      e.code === 1014 ||
      // test name field too, because code might not be present
      // everything except Firefox
      e.name === 'QuotaExceededError' ||
      // Firefox
      e.name === 'NS_ERROR_DOM_QUOTA_REACHED') &&
```

```
          // acknowledge QuotaExceededError only if there's something already stored
          storage.length !== 0;
      }
  },
  save: function(hash) {
    window.localStorage.setItem('hash', hash);
  },
  restore: function() {
    return window.localStorage.getItem('hash');
  },
  delete: function() {
    window.localStorage.removeItem("hash");
  }
}

:: Start
<%
  if(window.storage.ok()) { %>
  Window storage works!
<% } %>
<%
  if(window.storage.restore()) { %>
  There is a session saved!
<% } %>
[[Save the session hash?]]

[[Restore from previous session?]]

[[Delete previous session?]]

:: Save the session hash?
The hash is <%= window.story.saveHash() %>. It has been saved!

<% if(window.storage.ok()) {
  window.storage.save(window.story.saveHash())
}%>

[[Go back?|Start]]
```

:: Restore from previous session?
<% if(window.storage.ok()) {
    if(window.story.restore(window.storage.restore())) { %>
    The restore was successful!
<% }
}
%>

[[Go back?|Start]]

:: Delete previous session?
<% window.storage.delete() %>

[[Go back?|Start]]

Setting and Showing Variables

Summary

In Snowman, the *s* global variable can be used to store and retrieve values. Properties can be created and assigned freely. The Underscore template functionality can be used to define, change, and show the values of variables. The value of a variable can be shown by writing the name of that variable surrounded by **<%= %>** signs (as in the example below).

Twee Code

```
:: StoryTitle
Setting and Showing Variables in Snowman

:: Start
<%
   s.numberVariable = 5;
   s.wordVariable = "five";
   s.phraseVariable = "The value";
%>

<%= s.phraseVariable %> is <%= s.numberVariable %> and <%= s.wordVariable %>.

<%
   s.numberVariable++;
%>

<%= s.phraseVariable %> is <%= s.numberVariable %> and <%= s.wordVariable%>.
```

Space Exploration

Summary

Games in the roguelike genre often have random events that influence player choices. Depending on these random events, a player's decisions can have lasting impact or even lead to the end of a session of play.

Heavily inspired by *FTL: Faster Than Light* (2012), this example uses the **_.random()** function to generate a system of planets consisting of either RED, more risk and more reward, or GREEN, less risk and less reward. Upon entering a system of planets, the player can choose to visit these planets and receive different events based on the outcome of another **_.random()** function to select between several possible incidents. While traveling, the player must also balance the health of the ship, the number of jumps left, and the remaining fuel, which are all displayed using the **window.story.render()** function in combination with Underscore.js templates.

Twee Code

```
:: StoryTitle
Space Exploration in Snowman

:: UserScript[script]
// Create a global setup object
window.setup = window.setup || {};

// Add 'variables' object to setup
window.setup.variables = {};
var _vars = window.setup.variables;
_vars.health = 20;
_vars.fuel = 4;
_vars.system = [];
_vars.numberOfJumpsLeft = 10;

// Create global functions
```

```
window.setup.functions = {};
var _functions = window.setup.functions;

_functions.redOutcome = function() {
    var _vars = window.setup.variables;
    var _percentage = _.random(1, 10);
    var response = "";
    if( _percentage >= 6) {
       var _foundHealth = _.random( 1, 5);
       var _foundFuel = _.random( 1, 3);
       response = "The hostile environment damaged the ship, but extra fuel was found. -"
+ _foundHealth + " to health and +" + _foundFuel + " to fuel.";
        _vars.health -= _foundHealth;
        _vars.fuel += _foundFuel;

    } else {

        if( _percentage <= 3) {
          var _foundHealth = _.random(2, 7);
          response = "A hostile ship attacked. -" + _foundHealth + " to health";
         _vars.health -= _foundHealth;

      } else {
        response = "Nothing happened."
      }
    }

    return response;
};

 _functions.greenOutcome = function() {
    var _vars = window.setup.variables;
    var _percentage = _.random(1, 10);
    var response = "";
    if( _percentage == 1) {
       var _foundFuel = _.random( 1, 2);
       response = "Fuel was found in some wreckage. + " + _foundFuel + "to fuel";
        _vars.fuel += _foundFuel;

    } else {
```

```
        if( _percentage >= 6) {
          var _foundHealth = _.random(1, 3);
        response = "During a brief pause, the ship was able to be repaired. +" + _foundHealth + " to health";
          _vars.health += _foundHealth;

      } else {
        response = "Nothing happened."
      }
    }

    return response;
  };

:: Start
[[Explore Space|Explore Space 1]]

:: Explore Space 1
<div class="gameScreen">

  <% var _vars = window.setup.variables; %>
  <% _vars.fuel-- %>
  <% _vars.numberOfJumpsLeft-- %>

  [[ Hyperjump |Explore Space 2]]

  <div id="HUD">
    <%= window.story.render("HUD") %>
  </div>

  <%= window.story.render("Generate System") %>

  <div id="display"></div>

  <%= window.story.render("Display System") %>

  <%= window.story.render("Check Status") %>

</div>
```

```
:: Explore Space 2
<div class="gameScreen">

   <% var _vars = window.setup.variables; %>
   <% _vars.fuel-- %>
   <% _vars.numberOfJumpsLeft-- %>

   [[ Hyperjump |Explore Space 1]]

   <div id="HUD">
     <%= window.story.render("HUD") %>
   </div>

   <%= window.story.render("Generate System") %>

   <div id="display"></div>

   <%= window.story.render("Display System") %>

   <%= window.story.render("Check Status") %>

</div>

:: Generate System
<script>
   var _vars = window.setup.variables;

   var planets =_.random(1, 4);

   _vars.system = new Array(planets);

   for(var i = 0; i < _vars.system.length; i++) {
     _vars.system[i] = _.sample(["RED", "GREEN"]);
     }
</script>

:: Display System
<script>
   var _vars = window.setup.variables;
```

```
  // Wipe out current contents
  $("#display").html("");

  for(var i = 0; i < _vars.system.length; i++) {

    if(_vars.system[i] == "RED") {
    var link = $("<a href='#'>RED</a>")
    .click(function(e) {
        $( this )
      .replaceWith( window.story.render("Show Outcome - Red") );
      return false;
    });
    $("#display").append( link );
    $("#display").append( "<br>" );
    }

    if(_vars.system[i] == "GREEN") {
      var link = $("<a href='#'>GREEN</a>")
    .click(function(e) {
        $( this )
      .replaceWith( window.story.render("Show Outcome - Green") );
      return false;
    });
    $("#display").append( link );
    $("#display").append( "<br>" );
    }
  }

</script>

:: Show Outcome - Red
<%= window.setup.functions.redOutcome() %>
<% $("#HUD").html(window.story.render("HUD")) %>
<%= window.story.render("Check Status") %>


:: Show Outcome - Green
<%= window.setup.functions.greenOutcome() %>
<% $("#HUD").html(window.story.render("HUD")) %>
 <%= window.story.render("Check Status") %>
```

:: HUD
Health: <%= window.setup.variables.health %>
Fuel: <%= window.setup.variables.fuel %>
Number of Jumps Left: <%= setup.variables.numberOfJumpsLeft %>

:: Destroyed
The ship exploded in flight.

<h3>Game Over</h3>

:: Lost in space
Without fuel, the ship tumbled and spun in the endless black.

<h3>Game Over</h3>

:: Safe
After 10 hyperjumps, the ship left the hazardous area and called for help.

<h3>Success!</h3>

:: Check Status
```
<script>

  var _vars = window.setup.variables;

  var status = "";

  if(_vars.health <= 0) {
    status = window.story.render("Destroyed");
  }
  if(_vars.fuel <= 0) {
    status = window.story.render("Lost in space");
  }
  if(_vars.numberOfJumpsLeft <= 0) {
    status = window.story.render("Safe");
  }

  if(status != "") {
    $(".gameScreen").html(status);
  }
</script>
```

Static Healthbars

Summary

"Static Healthbars" demonstrates how to write HTML elements that use variable values. In this example, Underscore template functionality is used to create **\<progress\>** and **\<meter\>** elements.

Twee Code

```
:: StoryTitle
Static Healthbars in Snowman

:: Start
<%
  window.setup = {};
  window.setup.health = 80;
%>

Show a healthbar using a Progress element:
<%= '<progress value="' + window.setup.health + '" max="100"></progress>' %>

Show a healthbar using a Meter element:
<%= '<meter value="' + window.setup.health + '" min="0" max="100"></meter>' %>
```

Story and Passage API

Summary

Often, it can be useful to access information about about about a Story or another passage while the Story is running. The **window.story.passage()** function and *window.passage.name* property in Snowman allow for getting this type of information.

Twee Code

```
:: StoryTitle
Story and Passage API in Snowman

:: Start
The title of this story is "<%= window.story.name %>."

<%
  window.setup = {};
  window.setup.passage = window.story.passage("Storage");
%>

The name of the passage is "<%= setup.passage.name %>."

The source of the passage is "<%= setup.passage.source %>"

:: Storage
This is content in the storage passage!
```

Style Markup

Summary

Snowman uses a sub-set of markdown for in-line styling. Snowman does not support multi-line markdown variations.

Twee Code

```
:: StoryTitle
Style Markup in Snowman

:: Start
*Emphasis* or _Emphasis_.

**Strong emphasis** or __Strong emphasis__.

~~Strikethrough~~

1. First ordered list item
2. Another item

# H1
## H2
### H3
#### H4
##### H5
###### H6

Escaped code line.
Another line of code.
```

```
| Tables        | Are            | Cool          |
| ------------- |:-------------:| -------------:|
| col 3         | is             | right-aligned |
| col 2         | is             | centered      |
| col 1         | is             | left-aligned  |
```

> Blockquotes are useful.
> This line is part of the same quote.

Timed Passages

Summary

Made famous in *Queers in Love at the End of the World* (2013), "Timed Passages" uses the the **_.delay()** function to count seconds while checking if a timer has reached zero. If so, the **window.story.show()** function will immediately transition to another passage.

Twee Code

```
:: Start
There are <span class="time-left">10</span> seconds left.

<%
$(function() {
  var timeLeft = parseInt($('.time-left').text());

  function tick() {
    if (--timeLeft === 0) {
      story.show('World End');
    }
    else {
      $('.time-left').text(timeLeft);
    }

    _.delay(tick, 1000);
  }

  /* Start ticking. */

  _.delay(tick, 1000);
});
%>

:: World End
The world ended.
```

See Also

Snowman: Delayed Text (pg. 208), Typewritter Effect (pg. 276)

Timed Progress Bars

Summary

"Timed Progress Bars" creates a global *window.setup* object and function, **timedprogressbars()**. Using jQuery within the definition, the function creates outer and inner **<div>** elements with CSS classes defined in the Story Stylesheet. Using a combination of **setInterval()** and **setTimeout()**, a timer is created. The length and color of an inner **<div>** element is adjusted based on the remaining time each loop.

When the timer runs out, the function argument is run and the length of the inner **<div>** element is reduced to 0.

Twee Code

```
:: StoryTitle
Timed Progress Bars in Snowman

:: UserScript[script]
window.setup = window.setup || {};

/*

    Description: Show a dynamically-created "progress bar"
    that changes colors as its timer runs down.

    Arguments:
      duration: time in seconds
      width: CSS width
      functionToRun: the function to execute when the timer runs out

*/

setup.timedprogressbars = function(duration, width, functionToRun) {
```

```javascript
// Save or generate a default duration
var duration = (Number(duration) || 60) * 1000;

// Save or generate a width
var width = width || "100%";

// Generate a unique hash
var hash = Math.floor(Math.random() * 0x100000000).toString(16);

//  Create an outer ID
var outerId = "outer_" + hash;

// Create an inner ID
var innerId = "inner_" + hash;

// Create an outer div,
// add an ID,
// add a class,
// change the CSS width, and
// append to the output
var progressbar = $("<div>")
.attr("id", outerId)
.addClass("progress-bar")
.css('width', width)
.appendTo(".passage");

// Create an inner div,
// add an ID,
// add a class,
// change the CSS width, and
// append to the progressbar
var progressvalue = $("<div>")
.attr("id", innerId)
.addClass("progress-value")
.css('width', "100%")
.appendTo(progressbar);

// Create a function to convert into hexadecimal
var toHex = function(num) {
```

```javascript
    var res = Math.round(Number(num)).toString(16);
    return (res.length === 1 ? "0" + res : res);
};

// Watch for the :passagedisplay event once
jQuery(document).one("sm.passage.shown", function() {
  // Get the current time
  var timeStarted = (new Date()).getTime();

  // Save a reference to the setInterval function
  var workFunction = setInterval(function() {
          console.log('workFunction');

    // Check if the element is still 'connected'
    if(!progressbar.closest(document.documentElement)) {
      // Navigated away from the passage
      clearInterval(workFunction);
      return;
    }

    // Figure out how much time has passed
    var timePassed = (new Date()).getTime() - timeStarted;

    // Check if the timer has run out
    if(timePassed >= duration) {

      // Reduce the inner width to 0
      progressvalue.css('width', "0");

      // Clear interval
      clearInterval(workFunction);

      // Run the inner function (if set)
      setTimeout(functionToRun, 40);
      return;
    }

    // Update the progress percentage
    var percentage = 100 - 100 * timePassed / duration;
```

```
            // Save the new color
            var color = "#"
              + toHex(Math.min(255, 510 -  5.1 * percentage))
              + toHex(Math.min(255, 5.1 * percentage)) + "00";

            // Update the background color of the inner div
            progressvalue.css("backgroundColor", color);

            // Update the inner div width
            progressvalue.css("width", (100 - 100 * timePassed / duration) + "%");

      }, 40);

    });


:: UserStylesheet[stylesheet]
.progress-bar {
  position: relative;
  border: 1px solid #777;
  background: black;
  height: 1em;
}
.progress-value {
  position: absolute;
  top: 0;
  left: 0;
  height: 100%;
  background: #00ff00;
}

:: Start
<script>

  setup.timedprogressbars(5, "20em", function(){
    // Hide the progress bar
    $(".progress-bar").css("display", "none");
    // Display the result
    $("#results").text("Too late!");
  });
```

```
</script>

<div id="results"></div>
```

See Also

Snowman: Adding Functionality (pg. 196)

Turn Counter

Summary

"Turn Counter" demonstrates the use of the *window.story.history* array in keeping track of "turns" (number of passages visited). The *window.story.render()* function is used to "display" or otherwise include another passage at the start of each.

In this example, the *length* of the array *window.story.history* is compared to its modulo 24 value. Sometimes known as "wrap around," the modulus operator (%) is used to get the remainder of the number of "turns" (passages) divided by 24. This creates a clock where its value shows one of a series of strings representing "morning", "mid-morning", "afternoon", or "night."

By visiting other passages, the turn count is increased and the hour reaches 23 before being reset back to 0 before increasing again.

Twee Code

```
:: StoryTitle
Turn Counter in Snowman

:: Start
<%= window.story.render("Turn Counter") %>
Rooms:

[[Back Room]]

[[Left Room]]

[[Right Room]]

:: Back Room
<%= window.story.render("Turn Counter") %>
Rooms:
```

[[Left Room]]

[[Right Room]]

[[Front Room|Start]]

:: Left Room
<%= window.story.render("Turn Counter") %>
Rooms:

[[Right Room]]

[[Back Room]]

[[Front Room|Start]]

:: Right Room
<%= window.story.render("Turn Counter") %>
Rooms:

[[Left Room]]

[[Back Room]]

[[Front Room|Start]]

:: Turn Counter
<%
  var hour = window.story.history.length % 24;

  if(hour <= 8){%>
    It is morning.
  <%}
  if(hour > 8 && hour <= 12){%>
    It is mid-morning.
  <%}
  if(hour > 12 && hour <= 16){%>

```
    It is afternoon.
  <%}
  if(hour > 16){%>
    It is night.
  <%}
%>
```

Typewriter Effect

Summary

"Typewriter Effect" demonstrates how to create a delayed character-by-character effect. In Snowman, this is achieved using recursive calls to the *setTimeout()* function to repeat calls once every one second. A jQuery selector is used to find an element with the ID "typewriter" whose HTML content is updated with the text every second until it is fully shown.

Twee Code

```
:: StoryTitle
Typewriter Effect in Snowman

:: UserScript[script]
// Create a global setup object
window.setup = window.setup || {};

// Add a 'typewriter' object
setup.typewriter = {};

// Save an index of the string.
// Start at -1 because it will be increased
//  once (to 0) before the first character is shown.
setup.typewriter.index = -1;

// Allow users to set global text
setup.typewriter.text = "";

// Save a reference to the setTimeout call
setup.typewriter.timerReference = 0;

// Write text character by character to an element
//  with the ID "typewriter"
setup.typewriter.write = function(){
```

```
  // Test if the index is less than the text length
    if(setup.typewriter.index < setup.typewriter.text.length) {
      // Update the current text character-by-character
    $("#typewriter").html(
      $("#typewriter").html() + setup.typewriter.text[setup.typewriter.index]
    );
      // Increase the index
    setup.typewriter.index++;
      // Save the timeout reference
    setup.typewriter.timerReference = setTimeout(setup.typewriter.write, 1000);
  } else {
    // Clear out the timeout once index is greater than string length
    clearTimeout(setup.typewriter.timerReference);
    // Reset the index
    setup.typewriter.index = -1;
  }

}

:: Start
<div id="typewriter"></div>
<%
  setup.typewriter.text = "Hello, world!";
  setup.typewriter.write();
%>
```

See Also

Snowman: Delayed Text (pg. 208)

Variable Story Styling

Summary

"Variable Story Styling" demonstrates how to use the **toggleClass()** jQuery function to switch between two pre-defined style rule-sets. Used with the "body" selector, the entire page is selected and the classes toggled when the function is called.

Twee Code

```
:: StoryTitle
Variable Story Styling in Snowman

:: UserStylesheet[stylesheet]
.green {
  background: white;
    color: green;
}
.white {
  background: black;
    color: white;
}

:: Start
This text is green on a white background.
<%
  s.styling = "green";
  $("body").toggleClass(s.styling);
%>
[[Next Passage]]

:: Next Passage
This text is white on a black background.
<%
  s.styling = "white";
  $("body").toggleClass(s.styling);
%>
```

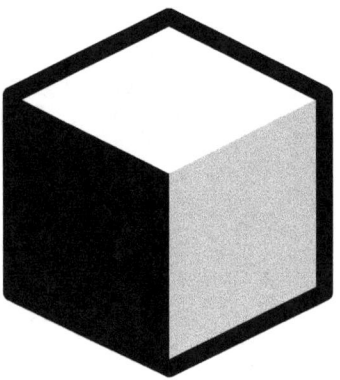

SugarCube

Adding Functionality

Summary

In SugarCube, additional functionality can be added through the *Macro.add()* function.

In this example, the *Date()* JavaScript function is used to get the current time. This is saved to *payload.contents*, and the *jQuery.wiki()* function is used to convert and append it to the current passage.

Twee Code

```
:: StoryTitle
Adding Functionality in SugarCube

:: UserScript[script]
Macro.add("currenttime", {
  tags: null,
  handler: function() {
    // Try the following code and catch any errors
    try {
      // Get the current time and save it to the payload
      this.payload.contents = new Date();

      // Wikify (and append) the current payload contents
      jQuery(this.output).wiki(this.payload.contents);

    } catch (ex) {
      // Return any errors
      return this.error("Error: " + ex.message);
    }
  }
});

:: Start
<<currenttime>><</currenttime>>
```

Arrays

Summary

Arrays are a collection of values. Each value in an array is assigned an *index*, which is a number that corresponds to the position of that item or element. Arrays have many built-in methods and other features, and SugarCube adds many more. Arrays can be created by assigning a variable to the array literal, which is a pair of brackets ([]): `<<set $myArray to []>>`.

Specific elements can be accessed in an array by following its variable name with a pair of brackets containing the index to check. Testing whether an array contains an element can be done using the **Array#includes()** function; adding new items can be done using the **Array#push()** function.

Twee Code

```
:: StoryTitle
Arrays in SugarCube

:: StoryInit
/% it is always a good idea to initialize your variables, but with arrays it is particularly important %/
<<set $inventory to []>>
<<set $chest to ['a shield', 'a suit of armor']>>
<<set $chestOpen to false>>

:: PassageHeader
You are currently carrying:
/% if the inventory contains nothing, show "nothing" %/\
<<if $inventory.length is 0>>\
    nothing.
<<else>>\
    /% the Array#join() method combines all array elements into a single string, with each element separated by the argument given %/\
    <<= $inventory.join(', ')>>.
<</if>>
-----
```

:: Start
/% we use the Array#push() method to add new items to our inventory array %/\
You find yourself inside a small room. In the corner, you see a sword, and decide to pick it up.

<<run $inventory.push('a sword')>>\
[[Continue|hallway]]

:: hallway
You see a chest here in the hallway. \
<<if not $chestOpen>>\
    Do you want to open it?

    <<link [[Open the chest.|chest]]>>
        /% concatenating the arrays and setting the result to $inventory moves all the items from the $chest array into the $inventory array %/
        <<set $inventory to $inventory.concat($chest)>>
        <<set $chestOpen to true>>
    <</link>>
<<else>>\
    It's open, and there's nothing inside.
<</if>>

[[Move on.|dart trap]]

:: chest
You open the chest and find <<= $chest.join(' and ')>>.

<<return "Okay.">>

:: dart trap
Several darts shoot out of a wall at you!
/% we can check to see if the player has a given item with Array#includes() %/
<<if $inventory.includes('a shield')>>\
    Luckily, your shield will protect you.
<<else>>\
    With no way to defend yourself, you die.
<</if>>

Audio

> **Information**
> This examples uses two additional files, **testpattern.ogg** and **testpattern.wav**. Both files need to be downloaded from the online Cookbook and placed in the same folder as the HTML file in order to work as designed.

Summary

SugarCube supports audio through multiple macros. For basic playing of audio, resources must be first cached through the **<<cacheaudio>>** macro and then can be referenced in others like the **<<audio>>** macro for playing and stopping.

Audio elements rely on sources either absolutely or relatively located. An absolute reference starts with HTTP or another protocol; a relative reference describes the location of the resource in relation to the webpage. Because audio files are external resources, they must also be accessed from a remote service, file hosting location, or stored separately with the webpage.

Due to browser differences in licensing, some audio formats are not universally supported. For best results in using audio in Twine, it is recommended to use multiple formats, allowing the browser to choose which format is best supported when first loaded.

Twee Code

```
:: StoryTitle
Audio in SugarCube

:: Start
<<link "Start audio!">>
  <<audio "testpattern" play>>
<</link>>

<<link "Stop audio!">>
  <<audio "testpattern" stop>>
```

```
<</link>>

:: StoryInit
<<cacheaudio "testpattern" "testpattern.ogg" "testpattern.wav">>
```

Conditional Statements

Summary

In SugarCube, the **<<if>>** and **<<else>>** macros conditionally run sections. If the statement is true, the **<<if>>** section will be run. Otherwise, the **<<else>>** section will be.

Twee Code

```
:: StoryTitle
Conditional Statements in SugarCube

:: Start
<<set $animal to "horse">>

<<if $animal is "dog">>
It's a dog!
<<else>>
It's a horse!
<</if>>
```

See Also

SugarCube: Setting and Showing Variables (pg. 338)

CSS Selectors

Summary

This example shows how to use CSS selectors to style different areas of the page. SugarCube uses nested **<div>**s with ids to structure its significant elements. Most notably the sidebar is a **<div>** with id "ui-bar". However, these elements are often more easily styled by other means, such as selecting the **<body>** element to style the entire page, and the "passage" class to style the current passage.

```
<body>
  <div id="ui-bar">...</div>
  <div id="story">
    <div id="passages">
      <div id="a-passage-name" class="passage">...</div>
    </div>
  </div>
</body>
```

Twee Code

```
:: StoryTitle
CSS Selectors in SugarCube

:: UserStylesheet [stylesheet]
body {
    background-color: darkgreen;
}

#ui-bar {
    border: 2px solid blue;
}

.passage {
    border: 1px solid red;
}
```

```
:: Start
The page has a green background; it contains this passage (red border) and the sidebar
(blue border).
[[Second]]

:: Second
This passage also has a red border.
```

See Also

Example of using a single class CSS selector to style a different element
SugarCube: Images (pg. 308)

Example of using two classes to style a single element
SugarCube: CSS and Passage Tags (pg. 290)

CSS and Passage Tags

Summary

This example shows how to use CSS selectors to style different passages based on how they are tagged. In SugarCube, the tag name is applied to both the **<body>** and the passage shown. To style different parts, use either the "body" selector or a combination of "passage" and the tag name.

SugarCube 2.x and later also applies a "data-tags" attribute to the **<html>**, **<body>**, and elements with the class "passage". These can also be used to style the page at different levels.

Twee Code

```
:: StoryTitle
CSS and Passage Tags in SugarCube

:: UserStylesheet[stylesheet]
/* Style the entire body when showing passage tagged with grey */
body.grey {
  color: green;
}

/* Style only the inner part of the passage tagged with "grey" */
.passage.grey {
  background: grey;
}

/* Style only the inner part of the passage tagged with "yellow" */
.passage.yellow {
  background: yellow;
  color: black;
}
```

:: Start[grey]
This passage has a grey background and green text.
[[Second]]

:: Second[yellow]
This passage has a yellow background and black text.

Cycling Choices

Summary

"Cycling Choices" demonstrates how to create a link which cycles through different choices when clicked on.

The cycle starts with the use of the **<<include>>** macro and assumption of *$choicesCount* beginning at the number -1. Within the passage "Cycling", the first 'cycle' begins with testing if the variable *$choices* exists. If it does not, *$choices* and *$choicesCount* are set (created) to their initial values.

Next, *$choicesCount* is then increased by one to the start value of 0 (the first location of an array in SugarCube) and the position of *$choices* is shown based on this.

If the user clicks on the link (created through using the **<<linkreplace>>** and **<<include>>** macros) again, future 'cycles' test if *$choicesCount* increases beyond the number of values in the *$choices* array and resets it to 0.

At the end of every cycle, the currently selected value is stored in the variable *$cyclingResult* for future access and usage.

Twee Code

```
:: StoryTitle
Cycling Choices in SugarCube

:: Start
Click options to cycle: <<include "Cycling">>
[[Submit|Results]]

:: Cycling
<<silently>>
<<if not $choices>>
  <<set $choicesCount to -1>>
```

```
    <<set $choices to ["First", "Second", "Third"]>>
<</if>>

<<set $choicesCount to $choicesCount + 1>>

<<if $choicesCount >= $choices.length>>
    <<set $choicesCount to 0>>
<</if>>

<<set $cyclingResult to $choices[$choicesCount]>>
<</silently>>
\<<linkreplace $choices[$choicesCount]>><<include "Cycling">><</linkreplace>>

:: Results
$cyclingResult
```

See Also

SugarCube: Modularity (pg. 321), Setting and Showing Variables (pg. 338)

Date and Time

Summary

"Date and Time" demonstrates how to use the JavaScript *Date()* functionality in SugarCube.

Twee Code

```
:: StoryTitle
Date and Time in SugarCube

:: Start
<<print "The current time (in milliseconds since January 1, 1970 00:00:00 UTC) is " + Date.now()>>

<<set $date to new Date()>>
The current month is <<print $date.getMonth() >>.
The current day is <<print $date.getDay() >>.
The current hour is <<print $date.getHours() >>.
The current minute is <<print $date.getMinutes() >>.
The current fullyear is <<print $date.getFullYear() >>.

<<set $originalDate to new Date("October 20, 2018")>>
<<set $timeDifference to Date.now() - $originalDate>>
It has been $timeDifference milliseconds since October 20, 2018.
```

Delayed Text

Summary

"Delayed Text" uses the **<<timed>>** macro to delay five seconds before showing text.

Twee Code

```
:: StoryTitle
Delayed Text in SugarCube

:: Start
<<timed 5s>>
It has been 5 seconds. Show the text!
<</timed>>
```

See Also

- **SugarCube: Typewriter Effect (pg. 357)**

Deleting Variables

Summary

In SugarCube, **<<unset>>** works as a "reverse" to **<<set>>**. Instead of setting a value, it deletes it. **<<unset>>** works on both temporary and story variables.

Twee Code

```
:: StoryTitle
SugarCube: Unsetting Variables

:: Start
<<set $proof to "hand-written letter">>

[[Accidentally drop the letter]]

:: Accidentally drop the letter
<<unset $proof>>

[[Present the letter to the sheriff]]

:: Present the letter to the sheriff
You present the $proof to the sheriff, not realizing the rain has washed away the ink from the hand-written letter.
```

See Also

SugarCube: Conditional Statements (pg. 287), Setting and Showing Variables (pg. 338)

Dice Rolling

Summary

"Dice Rolling" demonstrates how to create the same effects of rolling various physical dice through using the **random()** function and the **<<print>>** macro to show the results.

Twee Code

```
:: StoryTitle
SugarCube: Dice Rolling

:: Start
Rolling a 1d4: <<print random(1,4) >>
Rolling a 1d6: <<print random(1,6) >>
Rolling a 1d8: <<print random(1,8) >>
Rolling a 1d10: <<print random(1, 10) >>
Rolling a 1d12: <<print random(1, 12) >>
Rolling a 1d20: <<print random(1, 20) >>
Rolling a 1d100: <<print random(1, 100) >>
Rolling a 1d4 + 4: <<print random(1, 4) + 4 >>
Rolling a 1d6 - 2: <<print random(1, 6) - 2 >>
Rolling a 2d6 + 10: <<print random(1, 6) + random(1, 6) + 10 >>
```

Fairmath System

Summary

"Fairmath System" demonstrates how to re-create the Fairmath system found in ChoiceScript. Based on a percentage operation, increase and decrease changes the value by a percentage as the difference between the original and adjusted value.

This example uses the **<<widget>>** macro in SugarCube to separate operations for increasing and decreasing.

Twee Code

```
:: StoryTitle
Fairmath in SugarCube

:: Start
<!-- Fairmath formulas based on http://choicescriptdev.wikia.com/wiki/Arithmetic_operators#Fairmath -->

<<set $valueToAdjust to 100>>
The inital value is $valueToAdjust

<!-- Call the decrease widget -->
<<decrease $valueToAdjust 50>>
The adjusted value is $resultValue.

<!-- Save the changed value -->
<<set $valueToAdjust to $resultValue>>
<!-- Call the increase widget -->
<<increase $valueToAdjust 100>>
The adjusted value is $resultValue.

:: Fairmath Operations[widget]
<<widget "increase">>
```

```
<<set $resultValue to Math.round($args[0]+((100-$args[0])*($args[1]/100))) >>
<</widget>>

<<widget "decrease">>
<<set $resultValue to Math.round($args[0]-($args[0]*($args[1]/100) )) >>
<</widget>>
```

Geolocation

Summary

Many browsers allow access to the user's current location through the Geolocation property and associated functions. This functionality is subject to the user agreeing to allow access. Until the functionality is unlocked, or if the user declines, default values will be returned.

Functionality availability and their results should always be tested against other location services or information. Most browsers will return results through the fastest and sometimes least-accurate methods possible.

This example uses **<<linkreplace>>** and **<<script>>** macros to run JavaScript in passages in SugarCube. The *State.variables* object is used to store the results of running JavaScript functions and using those values in TwineScript.

Twee Code

```
:: StoryTitle
Geolocation in SugarCube

:: UserScript[script]
(function () {

  window.geolocation = {

    available: function() {
      return ("geolocation" in navigator
        && typeof navigator.geolocation.getCurrentPosition === "function");
    },
    getLocation: function() {

      // Create initial values
      var location = { latitude : 0, longitude : 0 };
```

```
    // Create success callback to store values
    var  positionSuccess = function (position) {

      location.latitude = position.coords.latitude;
      location.longitude = position.coords.longitude;

    };

    // Create error callback
    var positionError = function (error) {
      /* Code that handles errors */
    };

    // Create initial options
    var positionOptions = {
      timeout: 31000,
      enableHighAccuracy: true,
      maximumAge : 120000
    };


    // Ask for location based on callbacks and options
    navigator.geolocation.getCurrentPosition(
      positionSuccess,
      positionError,
      positionOptions
    );

    // Return location found
    // If not location, will return initial (0,0) values
    return location;

},
approximateLocation: function (a, b, allowedDiff) {
    // allowedDiff must always be > 0
  if (a === b) { // handles various "exact" edge cases
    return true;
  }
```

```
      allowedDiff = allowedDiff || 0.0005;

      return Math.abs(a - b) < allowedDiff;
    }

  };

}());

:: Start
<<linkreplace "Ask for permission">>
  <<script>>

  State.variables.geoLocationAvailable = window.geolocation.available();

  if(window.geolocation.available()) {
    State.variables.location = window.geolocation.getLocation();
  }
  <</script>>
  [[Show results]]
<</linkreplace>>



:: Show results
<<script>>

  State.variables.geoLocationAvailable = window.geolocation.available();

  if(window.geolocation.available()) {
    State.variables.location = window.geolocation.getLocation();
  }
<</script>>

Is geolocation available? $geoLocationAvailable

If so, what is the current location?

Latitude: $location.latitude
```

Longitude: $location.longitude

Are we in the approximate location of Stonehenge (51.1788853, -1.828409)?

<<set $approxLat to window.geolocation.approximateLocation(State.variables.location.latitude, 51.1788853) >>

<<set $approxLong to window.geolocation.approximateLocation(State.variables.location.longitude, -1.828409) >>

Latitude: $approxLat
Longitude: $approxLong

Google Fonts

Summary

"Google Fonts" uses a Google Font loaded via the CSS **@import** at-rule. A class style rule ("message") is then created using the imported font-family and applied to a **<div>** element within a single passage.

Other Google Fonts could be imported and applied using the same method, creating new class or ID style rules to be applied for and across different HTML elements in the same way.

Twee Code

```
:: StoryTitle
SugarCube: Google Fonts

:: StoryStylesheet[stylesheet]
@import url('https://fonts.googleapis.com/css?family=Roboto');

.message {
  font-family: 'Roboto', sans-serif;
}

:: Start
<div class="message">This text is styled using a Google Font</div>
```

Headers and Footers

Summary

"Headers and Footers" demonstrates the use of "PassageHeader" and "PassageFooter" special names for passages. When these special names are used, the 'Header' is prepended and the 'Footer' name is appended to all passages.

Twee Code

```
:: StoryTitle
SugarCube: Headers and Footers

:: Start
This is content between the header and the footer.

:: PassageHeader
This is the header!

:: PassageFooter
This is the footer!
```

See Also

SugarCube: Passage Events (pg. 324)

Hidden Link

Summary

"Hidden Link" demonstrates how to create a 'hidden' link that is only revealed when the cursor passes over it.

Using CSS and JavaScript, a rule is created for transparent color and applied or removed through using jQuery's **on()** function with 'mouseenter' and 'mouseleave' events.

The **postdisplay** functionality is also used to run JavaScript after each passage is displayed.

Twee Code

```
:: StoryTitle
SugarCube: Hidden Link

:: UserScript[script]
postdisplay['hidden-link-setup'] = function () {
  /*
    Hidden links that are always hidden:
      <span class="hidden">[[A hidden link]]</span>
  */
  $('.hidden')
    .addClass('hidden');

  /*
    Hidden links that hide unless you're hovering over them:
      <span class="hides">[[A hidden link]]</span>
  */
  $('.hides')
    .addClass('hidden')
    .on('mouseenter', function () {
      $(this).removeClass('hidden');
    })
```

```
      .on('mouseleave', function () {
        $(this).addClass('hidden');
      });

    /*
      Hidden links that reveal themselves when you hover over them:
        <span class="reveals">[[A hidden link]]</span>
    */
    $('.reveals')
      .addClass('hidden')
      .one('mouseenter', function () {
        $(this).removeClass('hidden');
      });
};


:: UserStylesheet[stylesheet]
.hidden a {
  color: transparent;
}


:: Start
A hidden link that's always hidden: <span class="hidden">[[A hidden link]]</span>

A hidden link that hides unless you're hovering over it: <span class="hides">[[A hidden link]]</span>

A hidden link that reveals itself when you hover over it: <span class="reveals">[[A hidden link]]</span>

:: A hidden link
You found it!
```

Images

Summary

When using SugarCube, images can be displayed through the image HTML element and **url()** CSS data type when encoded as Base64.

When using an image element, its source is either absolutely or relatively located. An absolute reference starts with HTTP or another protocol; a relative reference describes the location of the image in relation to the webpage.

Because images are external resources, they need to be included with the webpage as Base64-encoded or in another location. While Base64-encoded images can be embedded in a webpage, it also increases its overall size. External images require additional hosting and are included through their reference in CSS (URL) data type or image (SRC) attribute.

Many macros also support using images in SugarCube and their location can be used within wiki syntax. Base64-encoded images are not supported in wiki image syntax.

Twee Code

```
:: StoryTitle
Images in SugarCube

:: UserStylesheet[stylesheet]
.base64image {
  width: 256px;
  height: 256px;
  /* Base64 image truncated for example */
  /* See Twee file for full version. */
  background-image: url('data:image/png;base64...');
}
```

:: Start
This is an image element:

<img src="https://twinery.org/homepage/img/logo.svg" width="256" height="256">

This is a Base64-encoded CSS image background:

<div class="base64image"></div>

Importing External JavaScript

> **Information**
> The successful loading of an external JavaScript file or library commonly produces no visual output. The code within the example passage is not required for the successful loading of an external file or library.

Summary

"Importing External JavaScript" demonstrates how to import an externally stored JavaScript library, jQuery UI.

This example uses the SugarCube **importScripts()** function to load and integrate the script file's contents.

Twee Code

```
:: StoryTitle
SugarCube: Importing External JavaScript


:: UserScript [script]
/* Import the jQuery UI library. */
importScripts("https://ajax.googleapis.com/ajax/libs/jqueryui/1.12.1/jquery-ui.min.js");


:: Start
<p>Click on the grey box below to see it bounce.</p>
<div id="box" style="width: 100px; height: 100px; background: #ccc;"></div>
```

```
<<script>>
$(document).one(':passagerender', function (ev) {
  $(ev.content)
    .find("#box")
    .click(function () {
      $("#box").toggle("bounce", {times: 3}, "slow");
    });
});
<</script>>
```

Keyboard Events

Summary

"Keyboard Events" demonstrates how to capture keyboard events and then how to associate individual keys with activities within a story.

The example uses jQuery's **on()** function to monitor for all "keyup" events. Once a "keyup" event has occurred, two values are available:

- The *keyCode* property: the numerical value representing the key presented in its decimal ASCII code supported by effectively all browsers.
- The *key* property: the string value of the key presented supported by most modern web-browsers.

Twee Code

```
:: StoryTitle
SugarCube: Keyboard

:: UserScript[script]
(function () {
  $(document).on('keyup', function (ev) {
    /* the ev variable contains a keyup event object.
     *
     * ev.keyCode - contains the ASCII code of the key that was released, this property
is supported in effectively all browsers.
     * ev.key     - contains the key value of the key that was released, this property
is supported by most modern browsers.
     *
     */
```

```
      /* the following shows an alert when the 'a' key is released. */
      if (ev.key === 'a') {
        UI.alert("the 'a' key was released.");
      }
    });
  }());
```

:: Start
Press and release the "a" key to show an Alert dialog.

Left Sidebar

Summary

SugarCube has a built-in left sidebar whose contents can be changed by adding one of several special passages to your story.

The following list describes each of the special passages in the order that they appear vertically within the sidebar:

- StoryBanner appears directly above the story's Title. One use is to show the story's icon/image.
- StorySubtitle appears directly below the story's Title. One use is to show the story's version information.
- StoryAuthor is used to show the Author's information.
- StoryCaption is generally used to show dynamic information about the main character or the story's progress.
- StoryMenu appears directly above the *Save* button and is used to show custom menu items.
- StoryShare appears directly below the *Restart* button and is used to access a dialog containing Author's social media or web-site links.

The sidebar can be manually stowed (hidden) and unstowed (revealed) by selecting either the < or > icon in the sidebar's top right corner. The same effect can be achieved programmatically by using the UIBar global object and its **UIBar.stow()** and **UIBar.unstow()** functions.

Twee Code

```
:: StoryTitle
Left Sidebar in SugarCube

:: Start
<<set $name to "Jane Doe", $location to "Work">>\
[[Another passage]]
```

```
<<link "Stow the sidebar!">>
  <<run UIBar.stow() >>
<</link>>
<<link "Unstow the sidebar!">>
  <<run UIBar.unstow() >>
<</link>>


:: StoryBanner
<img src="https://twinery.org/homepage/img/logo.svg" width="64" height="64">


:: StorySubtitle
Version: 0.2.1


:: StoryAuthor
by Anonymous


:: StoryCaption
Name: $name
Location: $location


:: StoryMenu
[[New story link!|Start]]


:: StoryShare
[[Twinery|https://twinery.org/]]


:: Another passage
<<set $name to "John Smith", $location to "Shop">>\
[[Start]]
```

Loading Screen

Summary

"Loading Screen" demonstrates how the **LockScreen.lock()** and **LockScreen.unlock()** functions work in SugarCube. (This example also uses the **setTimeout()** JavaScript function.)

Twee Code

```
:: StoryTitle
Loading Screen in SugarCube

:: UserScript[script]
// Lock the screen and save the ID
var lockID = LoadScreen.lock();

// Pause for 5 second before unlocking the screen
setTimeout(function(){
    LoadScreen.unlock(lockID);
}, 5000);

:: Start
You can now see this after the long pause!
```

Lock and Key: Variable

> **Information**
> This example is affected by history changes in the story. Undoing or re-doing back to a passage containing this recipe has the potential to change its saved values.

Summary

"Lock and Key: Variable" demonstrates how to create the effect of picking up a key and unlocking a door. In this example, the key is a variable (*$key*) and is initially set to the value *false* in the Start passage.

When the link (created using a **<<linkreplace>>** macro) "Pick up the key" is clicked, *$key* is changed to the value *true* and the door link changes from its initial response of "Locked Door" to a link to the passage Exit.

Twee Code

```
:: StoryTitle
Lock and Key: Variable in SugarCube

:: Start
<<set $key to false>>

Rooms:
[[Back Room]]
[[Front Room]]

:: Front Room
<<if $key is true>>
    [[Exit]]
<<else>>
    Locked Door
<</if>>
```

Rooms:
[[Back Room]]

:: Back Room
<<if $key is false>>
    Items:
    <<linkreplace "Pick up the key">><<set $key to true>>You have a key.<</linkreplace>>
<<else>>
    There is nothing here.
<</if>>

Rooms:
[[Front Room]]

:: Exit
You found the key and went through the door!

See Also

SugarCube: Setting and Showing Variables (pg. 338)

Looping

Summary

In programming terminology, a "loop" is a common technique for iterating (moving through one by one) some type of data. In SugarCube, the control macro **<<for>>** provides this functionality. It acts like the **for** keyword in JavaScript and its usage works in a similar way.

In this example, the array *arrayInventory* is set to the series of strings "Bread", "Pan", and "Book". Using the **<<for>>** macro, a temporary variable is set to 0 and increased for each loop until its value is no longer less than the length (number of entries) of the array. Inside the macro, the text is shown each time with the value of the entry matching the position of the value of *_i* in the array substituted.

Twee Code

```
:: StoryTitle
Looping in SugarCube

:: Start
<!-- Set the variable $arrayInventory to the array containing "Bread", "Pan", "Book" -->
<<set $arrayInventory to ["Bread", "Pan", "Book"]>>

<!-- Set the temporary variable _l to 0 and increase it until it is greater than the
length of the array $arrayInventory -->
<<for _i to 0; _i lt $arrayInventory.length; _i++>>
You have $arrayInventory[_i]
<</for>>
```

Modal (Pop-up Window)

Summary

This example uses the built-in *Dialog* object to **setup()**, add content (**wiki()**), and finally **open()** the dialog window. SugarCube also comes with additional functionality to adjust other **dialog** settings.

Twee Code

```
:: StoryTitle
SugarCube: Modal

:: Start
<<link "Open dialog!">>
  <<script>>
    Dialog.setup("Dialog");
    Dialog.wiki("Text within the dialog window");
    Dialog.open();
  <</script>>
<</link>>
```

Modularity

Summary

In programming terminology, modularity refers to dividing software into different sections related to their purpose or to better organize the whole. In SugarCube, this technique can be used through the **<<include>>** macro to print the contents of one passage in another. Parts of a story can often be re-used in this way.

The **<<widget>>** macro offers a simplified way of creating new, custom macros using other SugarCube macros and TwineScript instead of JavaScript. When compared to **<<include>>**, widgets have the advantage of accepting arguments and expressions similar to the way other SugarCube macros can. New widgets must be added through passages with the tag **widget**.

Twee Code

```
:: StoryTitle
Modularity in SugarCube

:: Start
<<set $lineOne to "Give us a verse">>
<<set $lineTwo to "Drop some knowledge">>

<<include "showLineOne">>
<<include "showLineTwo">>

<<showLine 1>>
<<showLine 2>>

:: showLineWidget [widget]
<<widget 'showLine'>>\
    <<nobr>>
        <<if $args[0] is 1>>
            $lineOne
```

```
            <<elseif $args[0] is 2>>
                $lineTwo
            <</if>>
    <</nobr>>\
<</widget>>

:: showLineOne
$lineOne

:: showLineTwo
$lineTwo
```

Moving through a dungeon

Summary

"Moving through a 'dungeon'" uses a two-dimensional array for the "map" and two variables, X and Y, to track movement through the space. The 'Map System' passage checks the positions of X and Y relative to the "map" and writes the available directional movement options. Once a direction is clicked, the X and Y values are added or subtracted corresponding to the direction and the map is re-drawn again. Symbols are then placed on the map matching the walls, movement space, and player.

Twee Code

```
:: StoryTitle
SugarCube: Moving through a Dungeon

:: UserStylesheet[stylesheet]
#map {
    font-family: monospace;
}

:: Start
<<include "Map System">

:: StoryInit
<<set $mapArray to
[[0,0,0,0,0,0,0,0,0,0,0],
[0,1,1,1,0,1,1,1,1,1,0],
[0,0,0,1,0,0,0,0,0,1,0],
[0,1,0,1,1,1,1,1,0,1,0],
[0,1,0,0,0,0,0,1,0,1,0],
[0,1,1,1,1,1,1,1,0,1,0],
[0,0,0,0,0,0,0,1,0,1,0],
[0,1,0,1,1,1,1,1,1,1,0],
[0,1,0,1,0,0,0,1,0,0,0],
[0,1,1,1,0,1,1,1,1,2,0],
[0,0,0,0,0,0,0,0,0,0,0]]>>
```

```
<<set $positionX to 1>>
<<set $positionY to 1>>

:: Location
<span id="map">
<<nobr>>
<<for $i to 0; $i lt $mapArray.length; $i++>>
    <<for $k to 0; $k lt $mapArray[$i].length; $k++>>
        <<if $k eq $positionX and $i eq $positionY>>
            <<print "P">>
        <<elseif $mapArray[$i][$k] eq 1>>
            <<print ".">>
        <<elseif $mapArray[$i][$k] eq 0>>
            <<print "#">>
        <<elseif $mapArray[$i][$k] eq 2>>
            <<print "E">>
        <</if>>
    <</for>>
    <<print "<br>">>
<</for>>
<</nobr>>
</span>

:: East
<<set $positionX += 1>>
<<include "Map System">>

:: West
<<set $positionX -= 1>>
<<include "Map System">>

:: South
<<set $positionY += 1>>
<<include "Map System">>

:: North
<<set $positionY -= 1>>
<<include "Map System">>
```

```
:: Map System
<<include "Location">>
<<nobr>>
<<if $mapArray[$positionY-1][$positionX] eq 1>>
[[North]] |
<<elseif $mapArray[$positionY-1][$positionX] eq 2>>
[[Exit]] |
<</if>>
<<if $mapArray[$positionY][$positionX+1] eq 1>>
[[East]] |
<<elseif $mapArray[$positionY][$positionX+1] eq 2>>
[[Exit]] |
<</if>>
<<if $mapArray[$positionY+1][$positionX] eq 1>>
[[South]] |
<<elseif $mapArray[$positionY+1][$positionX] eq 2>>
[[Exit]] |
<</if>>
<<if $mapArray[$positionY][$positionX-1] eq 1>>
[[West]] |
<<elseif $mapArray[$positionY][$positionX-1] eq 2>>
[[Exit]] |
<</if>>
<</nobr>>

:: Exit
You have exited the map.
```

See Also

SugarCube: Conditional Statements (pg. 287), Modularity (pg. 321), Setting and Showing Variables (pg. 338)

Passage Events

Summary

SugarCube triggers different events as they happen to passages. Through using jQuery and its own JavaScript event handling, code can be added to work with other, existing functionalities.

In this example, the "passagestart" and "passagerender" events are shown. In the event progression, the 'passagestart' event occurs before the PassageHeader, prepending its content. The 'passagerender' happens after the PassageFooter, appending its content. Through the use of event handling, content is added before the PassageHeader and after the PassageFooter as an example of when events occur while presenting passages.

Twee Code

```
:: StoryTitle
Passage Events in SugarCube

:: UserScript[script]
/*
    Prepend the content of the passage "New Header" to every passage.

    This demonstrates that the 'passagestart' event comes before
     the PassageHeader prepending.
*/
$(document).on(':passagestart', function (eventObject) {
    var headerContent = Story.get("New Header").processText();
    $(eventObject.content).wiki(headerContent);
});

/*
    Append the content of the passage "New Footer" to every passage.

    This demonstrates that the 'passagerender' event comes after
     the PassageFooter appending.
*/
```

```
$(document).on(':passagerender', function (eventObject) {
    var footerContent = Story.get("New Footer").processText();
    $(eventObject.content).wiki(footerContent);
});

:: Start
[[Another passage]]

:: Another passage
[[Back to beginning|Start]]

:: New Header
This is added before the PassageHeader!

:: PassageHeader
This is the PassageHeader.

:: PassageFooter

This is the PassageFooter!

:: New Footer
This is added after the PassageFooter!
```

See Also

SugarCube: Headers and Footers (pg. 303)

Passages in Passages

Summary

In SugarCube, the contents of a passage can be shown in another passage through the use of the `<<include>>` macro. By using the name of an existing passage, that passage's contents will be included where the macro is called.

Twee Code

```
:: StoryTitle
SugarCube: Passages in Passages

:: Start
This is the Start passage!
<<include "Another">>

:: Another
And this is Another passage!
```

Render Passage to Element

Summary

In SugarCube, the function **setPageElement()** renders the contents of a passage into an element based on its *id*.

The event ":passagedisplay" is used in this example to guarantee that the passage has been rendered before acting. Calling the function **setPageElement()** inside a jQuery event listener then renders another passage into an existing element.

Twee Code

```
:: StoryTitle
SugarCube: Render Passage to Element

:: Start
<div id="hudID"></div>
<<script>>
  // Wait for the passage to be displayed
  $(document).one(':passagedisplay', function (ev) {
    // Render the passage named HUD into the element with id of "hudID"
    setPageElement("hudID", "HUD");
  });
<</script>>

:: HUD
<h1>This is the heads-up display!</h1>
```

Passage Transitions

Summary

SugarCube provides multiple ways to address passage transitions. To work with the existing functionality, the *Config.passages.transitionOut* variable can be set to change the property (height, width, opacity, etc) of the passage element or the amount of time to retain the outgoing passage before removing it with the default transition effect.

Through using jQuery event listeners, different functionalities can be triggered as part of normal passage events such as rendering or displaying content. For example, acting on the ":passagerender" event could be used to apply a jQuery effect on the incoming passage object.

Twee Code

```
:: StoryTitle
SugarCube: Passage Transitions

:: UserScript[script]
// Fade in content using jQuery Effects
// Hide and then fade in the content over 2000ms (2s)
$(document).on(':passageend', function (event) {
  $(".passage").hide(0).fadeIn(2000);
});

:: Start
[[Another passage]]

:: A third passage
No more content!

:: Another passage
[[A third passage]]
```

Passage Visits

Summary

In SugarCube, the global function **visited()** returns the number of times a passage has been visited over the course of the story. Combined with the **<<= >>** macro expression, the result of a global function can be written to a passage.

Twee Code

```
:: StoryTitle
SugarCube: Passage Visits

:: Start
How many times has the passage "Another Passage" been visited? <<= visited("Another Passage")>>

[[Another Passage]]

:: Another Passage
[[Start]]
```

Player Statistics

Summary

Some of the most popular mechanics from table-top role-playing games are those where the player must determine their in-game statistics and then use them to make decisions.

In this example, the **<<link>>** macro is used multiple times to replace content and adjust values, while checking if the values are higher than a target number. In a second passage, these values are used in combination with a random number between 1 to 6, mimicking the common mechanic of rolling 1d6 plus the value of a statistic to beat a target number.

Twee Code

```
:: StoryTitle
Player Statistics in SugarCube

:: Start
Empathy: \
<<link "[+]">>
  <<if $totalPoints gt 0>>
    <<set $empathy++>>
    <<set $totalPoints-->>
    <<replace "#empathyStat">><<print $empathy>><</replace>>
    <<replace "#pointsStat">><<print $totalPoints>><</replace>>
  <</if>>
<</link>>\
<<link "[-]">>
  <<if $empathy gt 0>>
    <<set $empathy-->>
    <<set $totalPoints++>>
    <<replace "#empathyStat">><<print $empathy>><</replace>>
    <<replace "#pointsStat">><<print $totalPoints>><</replace>>
  <</if>>
<</link>>
```

```
Intelligence: \
<<link "[+]">>
  <<if $totalPoints gt 0>>
    <<set $intelligence++>>
    <<set $totalPoints-->>
    <<replace "#intelligenceStat">><<print $intelligence>><</replace>>
    <<replace "#pointsStat">><<print $totalPoints>><</replace>>
  <</if>>
<</link>>\
<<link "[-]">>
  <<if $intelligence gt 0>>
    <<set $intelligence-->>
    <<set $totalPoints++>>
    <<replace "#intelligenceStat">><<print $intelligence>><</replace>>
    <<replace "#pointsStat">><<print $totalPoints>><</replace>>
  <</if>>
<</link>>
<<link "[Reset Points]">>
  <<set $empathy to 10>>
  <<set $intelligence to 10>>
  <<set $totalPoints to 5>>
  <<replace "#empathyStat">><<print $empathy>><</replace>>
  <<replace "#intelligenceStat">><<print $intelligence>><</replace>>
  <<replace "#pointsStat">><<print $totalPoints>><</replace>>
<</link>>

Empathy: <span id="empathyStat">10</span>
Intelligence: <span id="intelligenceStat">10</span>
Remaining Points: <span id="pointsStat">5</span>

[[Test Stats]]

:: StoryInit
<<set $empathy to 10>>
<<set $intelligence to 10>>
<<set $totalPoints to 5>>

:: Test Stats
<<linkreplace "Make an intelligence check?">>
```

```
  <<set _result to random(1, 6) + $intelligence >>
  <<if _result gte 15>>
  Intelligence Success! (_result >= 15)
  <<else>>
  Intelligence Failure! (_result < 15)
  <</if>>
<</linkreplace>>
<<linkreplace "Make an empathy check?">>
  <<set _result to random(1, 6) + $empathy >>
  <<if _result gte 15>>
  Emaphy Success! (_result >= 15)
  <<else>>
  Empathy Failure! (_result < 15)
  <</if>>
<</linkreplace>>
```

See Also

SugarCube: Conditional Statements (pg. 285), Setting and Showing Variables (pg. 336)

Programmatic Undo

Summary

While SugarCube supports allowing the user to undo and redo moves, the "undo" operation can also be accessed through the **<<back>>** macro. Through its use, changes from the most recent action can be "undone."

Twee Code

```
:: StoryTitle
Programmatic Undo in SugarCube

:: Start
[[Enter the Darkness]]

:: Enter the Darkness
<<back "You are not ready! Go back!">>
```

Saving Games

Summary

SugarCube provides built-in functionality for saving, viewing, and deleting game saves through its sidebar. However, the Save API also provides programmable access for re-creating this for users through functions like **Save.slots.has()***, **Save.slots.save()**, and ***Save.slots.load()**.

This example also demonstrates the use of the *State.variables* object to access variables in JavaScript and use them.

Twee Code

```
:: StoryTitle
Saving Games in SugarCube

:: Start
<<script>>
if (Save.slots.has(0)) {
  State.variables.slotA = true;
} else {
  State.variables.slotA = false;
}
<</script>>

<<if $slotA is true>>
  The first game slot exists! (This session was most likely reloaded from a game save.)
<</if>>

<<link "Save to the first slot?">>
  <<script>>
    if (Save.slots.ok()) {
      Save.slots.save(0);
    }
  <</script>>
<</link>>
```

```
<<link "Load from the first slot?">>
  <<script>>
    if (Save.slots.has(0)) {
      Save.slots.load(0);
    }
  <</script>>
<</link>>

<<link "Delete first slot and restart story?">>
  <<script>>
    if (Save.slots.has(0)) {
      Save.slots.delete(0);
      Engine.restart();
    }
  <</script>>
<</link>>
```

Setting and Showing Variables

Summary

Variables, symbols starting with **$** (for normal) or **_** (for temporary), can be "set" using the `<<set>>` macro in SugarCube.

$ is used for storing data throughout the story, and _ should be used for data only needed in the current passage. Using _ is useful for not wanting to accidentally overwrite variables elsewhere in the story. They can also help with debugging by not cluttering up the variables list of future passages. The value of a variable can be shown by writing the name of that variable in the body of a passage (as in the example below).

Twee Code

```
:: StoryTitle
Setting and Showing Variables in SugarCube

:: Start
<<set $numberVariable to 5>>
<<set $wordVariable to "five">>
<<set $phraseVariable to "The value">>

$phraseVariable is $numberVariable and $wordVariable.

<<set $numberVariable to $numberVariable + 1>>

$phraseVariable is $numberVariable and $wordVariable.
```

Space Exploration

Summary

Games in the roguelike genre often have random events that influence player choices. Depending on these random events, a player's decisions can have lasting impact or even lead to the end of a session of play.

Heavily inspired by *FTL: Faster Than Light* (2012), this example uses the **random()** function to generate a system of planets listed as either RED, more risk and more reward, or GREEN, less risk and less reward. Upon entering a system of planets, the player can choose to visit these planets and receive different events based on the outcome of another **random()** function to select between several possible incidents. While traveling, the player must also balance the health of the ship, the number of jumps left, and the remaining fuel, which are all displayed using the **<<include>>** macro. Finally, to capture the permanence of death in many roguelike games, the **<<goto>>** macro is used to prevent the use of the undo operation to navigate away from the death screen.

To cleanly present the text, this example also uses both the **<<silently>>** macro, to disregard all output, and **<<nobr>>** macro, to collapse the whitespace.

Twee Code

```
:: StoryTitle
Space Exploration in SugarCube

:: Start
[[Explore Space|Explore Space 1]]

:: StoryInit
<<set $health to 20>>
<<set $fuel to 4>>
<<set $system to [] >>
<<set $numberOfJumpsLeft to 10>>
```

```
:: Explore Space 1
<<link "Hyperjump">>
   <<set $fuel to $fuel - 1>>
   <<set $numberOfJumpsLeft to $numberOfJumpsLeft - 1>>
   <<goto "Explore Space 2">>
<</link>>

<div id="HUD">
   <<include "HUD">>
</div>

<<include "Generate System">>
<<include "Display System">>

:: Explore Space 2
<<link "Hyperjump">>
   <<set $fuel to $fuel - 1>>
   <<set $numberOfJumpsLeft to $numberOfJumpsLeft - 1>>
   <<goto "Explore Space 1">>
<</link>>

<div id="HUD">
   <<include "HUD">>
</div>

<<include "Generate System">>
<<include "Display System">>

:: Generate System
<<silently>>
   <<set _planets to random(1, 4) >>

   <<set $system to new Array(_planets) >>

   <<for _i to 0; _i lt _planets; _i++>>
      <<set $system[_i] to either("RED", "GREEN") >>
   <</for>>

<</silently>>
```

:: Display System
<<nobr>>
   <<for _i to 0; _i lt $system.length; _i++>>
     <<if $system[_i] eq "RED">>
        <<linkreplace $system[_i]>>
          <<include "Show Outcome - Red">>
        <</linkreplace>>
     <</if>>
     <<if $system[_i] eq "GREEN">>
        <<linkreplace $system[_i]>>
          <<include "Show Outcome - Green">>
        <</linkreplace>>
     <</if>>

   <</for>>
<</nobr>>

:: Show Outcome - Red
<<nobr>>
   <<set _percentage to random(1, 10) >>

   <<if _percentage gte 6>>

     <<set _foundHealth to random(1, 5) >>
     <<set _foundFuel to random(1, 3) >>

   The hostile environment damaged the ship, but extra fuel was found. (-_foundHealth to health and +_foundFuel to fuel)

     <<set $health to $health - _foundHealth >>
     <<set $fuel to $fuel + _foundFuel >>

   <<elseif _percentage lte 3>>

     <<set _foundHealth to random(2, 7) >>

   A hostile ship attacked. (-_foundHealth to health)

     <<set $health to $health - _foundHealth >>

```
    <<else>>
      Nothing happened.
    <</if>>

    <<replace "#HUD">>
      <<include "HUD">>
    <</replace>>

<</nobr>>

:: Show Outcome - Green
<<nobr>>
    <<set _percentage to random(1, 10)>>

    <<if _percentage eq 1>>

      <<set _foundFuel to random( 1, 2)>>

      Fuel was found in some wreckage. (+_foundFuel to fuel)

      <<set $fuel to $fuel + _foundFuel>>

    <<elseif _percentage gte 6>>

      <<set _foundHealth to random( 1, 3) >>

      During a brief pause, the ship was able to be repaired. (+_foundHealth to health)

      <<set $health to $health + _foundHealth>>

    <<else>>
      Nothing happened.
    <</if>>

    <<replace "#HUD">>
      <<include "HUD">>
    <</replace>>

<</nobr>>
```

:: HUD
Health: $health
Fuel: $fuel
Number of Jumps Left: $numberOfJumpsLeft
<<include "Check Status">>

:: Destroyed
The ship exploded in flight.

!!!Game Over.

:: Lost in space
Without fuel, the ship tumbled and spun in the endless black.

!!!Game Over

:: Safe
After 10 hyperjumps, the ship left the hazardous area and called for help.

!!!Success!

:: Check Status
<<nobr>>
  <<if $health lte 0>>
    <<goto "Destroyed">>
  <</if>>
  <<if $fuel lte 0>>
    <<goto "Lost in space">>
  <</if>>
  <<if $numberOfJumpsLeft lte 0>>
    <<goto "Safe">>
  <</if>>
<</nobr>>

Static Healthbars

Summary

"Static Healthbars" demonstrates how to write HTML elements that use variable values. In this example, Attribute Directive markup is used to inject the current value of the *$health* story variable into the **<progress>** and **<meter>** elements.

Twee Code

```
:: StoryTitle
Static Healthbars for SugarCube

:: Start
<<set $health to 80>>

Show a healthbar using a Progress element:
<progress @value="$health" max="100"></progress>

Show a healthbar using a Meter element:
<meter @value="$health" min="0" max="100"></meter>
```

Story and Passage API

Summary

Often, it can be useful to access information about a Story or another passage while the Story is running. The Story and Passage APIs in SugarCube allow for getting this type of information.

Twee Code

```
:: StoryTitle
Story and Passage API in SugarCube

:: Start
The title of this story is "<<print Story.title >>."

<<set $passage to Story.get("Storage")>>

The title of the passage is "<<print $passage.title>>."

The text of the passage is "<<print $passage.text >>"


:: Storage
This is content in the storage passage!
```

Style Markup

Summary

In SugarCube, style markup follows initial rules established in earlier versions of Twine while also adding many new ones.

Twee Code

```
:: StoryTitle
Style Markup in SugarCube

:: Start
//Emphasis//
''Strong Emphasis''
==Strikethrough==
Super^^script^^
Sub~~script~~
> Quote
>> Nested quote
* A list item
* Another list item
# A list item
# Another list item
"""No //format//"""
@@Highlight Inline@@
!Level 1 Heading
!!Level 2 Heading
!!!Level 3 Heading
!!!!Level 4 Heading
!!!!!Level 5 Heading
!!!!!!Level 6 Heading
```

Templates

Summary

Starting in SugarCube 2.29, Templates can be used to create a new special type of value that looks like a variable but acts like a macro. Templates follow the same rules as variables (limited to letters, numbers, and the underscore), but they start with the question mark, **?**, and can contain a hyphen in their name.

> **Note:** Templates are added using the Template API in SugarCube. They must be defined *before* they appear in a story.

This example also uses the **StoryInit** special passage name with the **<<script>>** macro to create a template before the first passage is shown.

Twee Code

```
:: StoryTitle
SugarCube: Templates

:: Start
You see a pirate before you.

Pirate: "?pirate"

:: StoryInit
<<script>>
Template.add('pirate', function () {
  return "Hello, me hardy!";
});
<</script>>
```

Timed Passages

Summary

Made famous in *Queers in Love at the End of the World* (2013), "Timed Passages" uses the the `<<repeat>>` macro to count seconds while checking if a timer has reached zero. If so, the `<<goto>>` macro will immediately transition to another passage.

Twee Code

```
:: StoryTitle
SugarCube: Timed Passages

:: StoryJavaScript[script]
UIBar.destroy();

:: Start
[[Start Timer|First Passage]]

:: Timer
<span id="countdown">The world will end in $seconds seconds.</span>
<<silently>>
    <<repeat 1s>>
        <<set $seconds to $seconds - 1>>
        <<if $seconds gt 0>>
            <<replace "#countdown">>The world will end in $seconds seconds.<</replace>>
        <<else>>
            <<replace "#countdown">><</replace>>
            <<goto "World End">>
            <<stop>>
        <</if>>
    <</repeat>>
<</silently>>
```

```
:: First Passage
<<include "Timer">>

[[Second Passage]]

:: Second Passage
<<include "Timer">>

[[First Passage]]

:: World End
The world has ended.

:: StoryInit
<<set $seconds to 10>>
```

See Also

SugarCube: Delayed Text (pg. 293), Typewritter Effect (pg. 355)

Timed Progress Bars

Summary

"Timed Progress Bars" uses the **Macro.Add()** function in SugarCube to introduce a new macro. Using jQuery within the definition, the new macro records arguments passed to it and creates outer and inner <div> elements with classes defined in the Story Stylesheet. Using a combination of **setInterval()** and **setTimeout()**, a timer is created based on the argument passed to the macro. The length and color of an inner <div> element is adjusted based on the remaining time each loop.

When the timer runs out, the *payload* of the macro is run and the length of the inner <div> element is reduced to 0.

Twee Code

```
:: StoryTitle
Timed Progress Bars in SugarCube

:: UserScript[script]
/*
    Macro: timedprogressbar

    Description: Show a dynamically-created "progress bar"
    that changes colors as its timer runs down.

    Original design: Akjosch (https://github.com/Akjosch)

    Arguments:
      [0]: The time to run in seconds
      [1]: The length of the progress bar in CSS units (px, em, or %)
*/
Macro.add("timedprogressbar", {
  isAsync : true,
  tags: null,
```

```
handler: function() {
  // Filter the payload for newlines and save it for later execution
  var payload = this.payload[0].contents.replace(/\n$/, '').trim();

  // Save or generate a default duration
  var duration = (Number(this.args[0]) || 60) * 1000;

  // Save or generate a width
  var width = this.args[1] || "100%";

  // Generate a unique hash
  var hash = Math.floor(Math.random() * 0x100000000).toString(16);

  //  Create an outer ID
  var outerId = "outer_" + hash;

  // Create an inner ID
  var innerId = "inner_" + hash;

  // Create an outer div,
  // add an ID,
  // add a class,
  // change the CSS width, and
  // append to the output
  var progressbar = $("<div>")
  .attr("id", outerId)
  .addClass("progress-bar")
  .css('width', width)
  .appendTo(this.output);

  // Create an inner div,
  // add an ID,
  // add a class,
  // change the CSS width, and
  // append to the progressbar
  var progressvalue = $("<div>")
  .attr("id", innerId)
  .addClass("progress-value")
  .css('width', "100%")
  .appendTo(progressbar);
```

```
// Create a function to convert into hexadecimal
var toHex = function(num) {
  var res = Math.round(Number(num)).toString(16);
  return (res.length === 1 ? "0" + res : res);
};

// Save a reference to possible payload content
var functionToRun = this.createShadowWrapper(
  payload
    ? function() { Wikifier.wikifyEval(payload); }
    : null
);

// Watch for the :passagedisplay event once
jQuery(document).one(":passagedisplay", function() {

  // Get the current time
  var timeStarted = (new Date()).getTime();

  // Save a reference to the setInterval function
  var workFunction = setInterval(function() {

    // Check if the element is still 'connected'
    if(! progressbar.prop("isConnected") ) {

      // Navigated away from the passage
      clearInterval(workFunction);
      return;
    }

    // Figure out how much time has passed
    var timePassed = (new Date()).getTime() - timeStarted;

    // Check if the timer has run out
    if(timePassed >= duration) {

      // Reduce the inner width to 0
      progressvalue.css('width', "0");
```

```
            // Clear interval
            clearInterval(workFunction);

            // Run the inner function (if set)
            setTimeout(functionToRun, 40);
            return;
          }

          // Update the progress percentage
          var percentage = 100 - 100 * timePassed / duration;

          // Save the new color
          var color = "#"
            + toHex(Math.min(255, 510 -  5.1 * percentage))
            + toHex(Math.min(255, 5.1 * percentage)) + "00";

          // Update the background color of the inner div
          progressvalue.css("backgroundColor", color);

          // Update the inner div width
          progressvalue.css("width", (100 - 100 * timePassed / duration) + "%");

       }, 40);

     });
   },
});


:: UserStylesheet[stylesheet]
.progress-bar {
  position: relative;
  border: 1px solid #777;
  background: black;
  height: 1em;
}
```

```
.progress-value {
  position: absolute;
  top: 0;
  left: 0;
  height: 100%;
  background: #00ff00;
}

:: Start
<<timedprogressbar 5 20em>>
  <<run UI.alert("Too late!")>>
<</timedprogressbar>>
```

See Also

Adding Functionality

> **SugarCube: Adding Functionality (pg. 280)**

Turn Counter

Summary

"Turn Counter" demonstrates the use of the *State.turns* attribute of the *State* object to keep track of the "turns" (moments within the story).

In this example, the *State.turns* property is compared to its modulo 24 value. Sometimes known as "wrap around," the modulus operator (%) is used to get the remainder of the number of "turns" (moments) divided by 24. This creates a clock where its value shows one of a series of strings representing "morning", "mid-morning", "afternoon", or "night."

This example also uses the special name "PassageHeader" as a named passage that is prepended to each passage in the story. The results of the modulo 24 calculation and clock string is displayed on every passage. By visiting other passages, the turn count is increased and the hour reaches 23 before being reset back to 0 before increasing again.

Twee Code

```
:: StoryTitle
SugarCube: Turn Counter

:: Start

Rooms:
[[Back Room]]
[[Left Room]]
[[Right Room]]

:: Back Room

Rooms:
[[Left Room]]
[[Right Room]]
[[Front Room|Start]]
```

:: Left Room

Rooms:
[[Right Room]]
[[Back Room]]
[[Front Room|Start]]

:: Right Room

Rooms:
[[Left Room]]
[[Back Room]]
[[Front Room|Start]]

:: PassageHeader
<<set $hour to State.turns % 24>>
<<if $hour <= 8>>It is morning.<</if>>
<<if $hour > 8 and $hour <= 12>>It is mid-morning.<</if>>
<<if $hour > 12 and $hour <= 16>>It is afternoon.<</if>>
<<if $hour > 16>>It is night.<</if>>

Typewriter Effect

Summary

SugarCube (versions ≥ 2.32.0) includes a **<<type>>** macro for creating a typing effect for displayed text. Almost any type of content can be typed using this macro, including links, styling markup, and other macros that display text.

Twee Code

```
:: StoryTitle
Typewriter Effect in Sugarcube

:: Start
<<type 60ms>>\
Hello world!

<<link "Click here!">><</link>>
\<</type>>
```

See Also

- **SugarCube: Delayed Text (pg. 293)**

Variable Story Styling

Summary

"Variable Story Styling" demonstrates how to use the **<<toggleClass>>** macro to switch between two pre-defined style rule-sets. Combined with the "body" selector, the entire page is selected and the classes are switched when the macro is used.

Twee Code

```
:: StoryTitle
Variable Story Styling in SugarCube

:: UserStylesheet[stylesheet]
.green {
  background: white;
    color: green;
}
.white {
  background: black;
    color: white;
}

:: Start
<<set $classToShow to "green">>
This text is green on a white background.
<<toggleclass "body" $classToShow>>
[[Next Passage]]

:: Next Passage
<<set $classToShow to "white">>
This text is white on a black background.
<<toggleclass "body" $classToShow>>
```

Using Add-ons

Summary

Many people have developed external add-ons for use in Story Formats like SugarCube. Often, these add-ons will come with instructions that should be followed to incorporate them into a story.

This example uses the **<<cyclinglink>>** macro created by Thomas Michael Edwards based on the work done by Leon Arnott for Twine 1. Its code was copied into the Story JavaScript for use in the story.

Twee Code

```
:: StoryTitle
Using Add-ons in SugarCube

:: UserScript[script]
/*! <<cyclinglink>> macro for SugarCube 2.x */
!function(){"use strict";if("undefined"==typeof version||"undefined"==typeof version.
title||"SugarCube"!==version.title||"undefined"==typeof version.major||version.major<2)
throw new Error("<<cyclinglink>> macro requires SugarCube 2.0 or greater, aborting
load");version.extensions.cyclinglinkMacro={major:3,minor:3,revision:2},macros.
cyclinglink={handler:function(a,b,c){function toggleText(w){w.classList.
remove("cyclingLinkInit"),w.classList.toggle(rl+"Enabled"),w.classList.
toggle(rl+"Disabled"),w.style.display="none"===w.style.display?"inline":"none"}
var rl="cyclingLink";switch(c[c.length-1]){case"end":var end=!0;c.
pop();break;case"out":var out=!0;c.pop()}var v=null;c.length&&"$"===c[0]
[0]&&(v=c[0].slice(1),c.shift());var h=State.variables;if(!out||!v||""!==h[v])
{var l=insertElement(a,"a");l.className="link-internal cyclingLink",l.
setAttribute("data-cycle",0);for(var i=0;i<c.length;i++){var on=i===(v?Math.
max(c.indexOf(h[v]),0):0),d=insertElement(null,"span",null,"cyclingLinkInit
cyclingLink"+(on?"En":"Dis")+"abled");on?(v&&(h[v]=c[i]),l.setAttribute("data-
cycle",i)):d.style.display="none",insertText(d,c[i]),on&&end&&i===c.length-1?l.
parentNode.replaceChild(d,l):l.appendChild(d)}jQuery(l).ariaClick(function(){var t=this.
```

```
childNodes,u=this.getAttribute("data-cycle")-0,m=t.length;if(toggleText(t[u]),u+=1,
out&&u===m?v&&(h[v]=""):(u%=m,v&&(h[v]=c[u])),(end||out)&&u===m-(end?1:0)){if(!end)
return void this.parentNode.removeChild(this);var n=this.removeChild(t[u]);return
n.className=rl+"End",n.style.display="inline",void this.parentNode.replaceChild(n,this)}
toggleText(t[u]),this.setAttribute("data-cycle",u)})}}}}();

:: Start
<<cyclinglink "First" "Second" "Third">>
```

www.ingramcontent.com/pod-product-compliance
Lightning Source LLC
LaVergne TN
LVHW081539070526
838199LV00057B/3721